From
The
Family
Kitchen

From The Family Kitchen

Discover Your Food Heritage and Preserve Favorite Recipes

Enjoy your discoveries!

by GENA PHILIBERT-ORTEGA

FAMILY
TREE
BOOKS

Cincinnati, Ohio
shopfamilytree.com

contents

Introduction

Food. I know what you're thinking: *What does food have to do with genealogy?* For me, the real question is why doesn't everyone include food traditions in their family history?

I have always loved genealogy. As a child I listened to my maternal grandmother talk about her life and the lives of her ancestors, and I have been listening to the stories told by family members ever since. I was one of those kids who would rather eavesdrop on adults as they reminisce than go out and play with my peers. Stories about the stuff of everyday life are so vital to genealogy. The everyday lives of our ancestors are exciting to hear about; the names and dates on charts, not so much. What's more everyday than food? That's why food is essential to genealogy.

I've also always been interested in the lives and roles of women throughout history. Most genealogists have trouble tracing female ancestors. Let's face it, women's history researchers have been writing for decades that women are overlooked by historians. Their lives are often relegated to the home. They lose their identity upon marriage and subsequent marriages when they change their surnames. It's not uncommon to look at a death certificate and in the place reserved for the name of the mother of the deceased there is the word *unknown*.

As I started teaching about ways to research female ancestors, it occurred to me that instead of feeling frustrated that women don't always appear in traditional genealogical resources, we should be looking at activities women participated in and how those activities left records of women's lives. In addition, we should be enhancing our research with social history. Social history tells us what life was like for everyday people during certain time periods. Just as many of us remember what we were doing when President John F. Kennedy was shot, the activities of our ancestors' days influenced their lives.

Now, don't get me wrong, this is not a book solely about researching female ancestors. Everyone eats, and children and husbands help prepare family meals. But the tools found in this book can help you round out the research on your foremothers.

Along with genealogy, I've always been interested in food. Not just in the eating of food but in what other people eat, how they prepare it, and the history behind it. Ever since I received *The Nancy Drew Cookbook* when I was a young girl, I've been fascinated with how food tells a story.

My love of food crops up even now. One of my favorite types of Facebook posts is when people add photographs on their Facebook walls of what they had to eat. My family and friends have been known to send me photos of what they just ordered at a restaurant or their latest creation. This hunger, excuse the pun, probably stems back to my parents, who would go out to eat when I was a child and bring me back the empty shells and crab claws from their dinners. This was truly exciting to me, imagining all of the different types of food people

enjoyed. Eating is such a seemingly mundane, ordinary experience, but it really isn't. Anyone who travels gets a sense of how food is different depending on where you live. And that's not taking into account other factors like ethnicity, religion, taste, and family influence. That's what this book is about. The seemingly everyday act of eating provides us with information to preserve our present-day family history and the food traditions established before we were born.

This book is different from most genealogy books. In it, we explore the lives of our ancestors through the food they ate. This information is meant to complement the genealogy research that you are already conducting. This approach is an attempt to get past just names and dates and learn more about our ancestors and the lives they led. My hope is that this books will encourage you to do two things: First, learn more about what your families ate and the food traditions they carried with them; second, record your own food history, a history that will interest generations of your family to come.

Enjoy your food discoveries.

Discover Your Family's

PART

I

Food Heritage

CHAPTER 1

Food Heritage

"Tell me what you eat, and I will tell you what your are."
—JEAN ANTHELME BRILLAT-SAVARIN

The Jean Anthelme Brillat-Savarin quote at the beginning of this chapter is well-known to fans of the cable television show *Iron Chef*. Penned by a French lawyer and politician, these words hold a grain of truth for family historians. What we eat is a reflection of so many things—including regionalism, ethnicity, and religion—and we want to learn more about these aspects of our ancestors' lives. What we eat can say a lot about us as individuals and as members of families.

This book explores the connection between family history, food history, and food tradition. What does food have to do with your genealogical research? Everything. Food plays a major role in social history. Adding a social history perspective to your family history will teach you more about who your ancestors really were. And when we pass on family food traditions to our children and grandchildren, we help them better understand their connection to their family history.

Social History and Your Ancestors

Family history is sometimes pursued with a very narrow lens. Too often, research is done solely to gather facts like names, dates, and places. Family history presented this way can seem like a middle school history class, the one that you could barely stay awake for. Most genealogists lament the lack of interest that their family, especially children and grandchildren, shows in the family history they are working so hard to uncover. Is it any wonder that the younger generation would have little interest in looking exclusively at names and dates printed on a pedigree chart or a family group sheet? Those names, dates, and places tell us very little about the lives of our ancestors. They are random facts in a larger story that is begging to be told.

At its best, family history is the story of our ancestors' tragedies, triumphs, sorrows, and happiness. Family history research and writings should include the everyday elements of our ancestors' lives, like what they wore, what type of house they lived in, what they learned in school, and what foods they ate. This type of detail illustrates how their everyday lives were similar to, or very different from, our own.

Adding social history information to your genealogy takes your research to the next level, past the gathering of names and dates. While we could spend all our time gathering thousands of names to add to our family trees, a social history approach allows us to add depth and layers to our family histories. Traditional history is written on a macro level of governments, leaders, and battles. Social history brings these events down to the micro level, the level of the everyman and woman, showing us how our ancestors' everyday lives were affected by the government, the leaders, and the wars of their times. Social history is concerned with ordinary people's everyday lives. As genealogist Katherine Scott Sturdevant writes in her book, *Bringing Your Family History to Life Through Social History*, "Social history is the study of ordinary people's extraordinary lives."[1]

Social history helps us connect the what and why with the who and where. It is only through the addition of social history, the so-called "putting the flesh on the bones" of our ancestors, that we learn who they were, what types of lives they lived, and what those lives have to say to us today.

Adding social history to an ancestor's life can mean looking at an ancestor's occupation and exploring the tools he used to make his living. Maybe you are interested in what education looked like for a seventeenth-century ancestor living in colonial America. Your ancestors' religion is something you may want to explore, researching what they believed and how they put that belief into action. A social history perspective can also mean trying to better understand the everyday routine of an ancestor's life. Today women with children spend their days multitasking as they cook meals, prepare children for the school day, run errands, work outside of the home, and complete household chores. Do you ever wonder what activities filled the days of your female ancestors? How did they do their shopping? What kind of houses did they live in? What did their clothes look like? How did they prepare for important events like weddings, childbirth, or even funerals? What kind of food did they eat and how did they procure and prepare it?

WHAT DID MY ANCESTORS EAT?

Food history and food traditions play a key role in social history. Remember the saying "You are what you eat." It's as applicable today as it was one hundred years ago. Understanding your family's food history and food traditions can help you learn more about your family's cultural identity, financial status, religious beliefs, and overall health. Some of your food history involves the happy times and celebrations and fond memories, while other aspects of your history may involve foods that helped people survive difficult times.

How is the food you eat every day different from what you eat during holidays or celebrations? Holidays and celebrations may mean an abundance of different kinds of foods that you may not necessarily eat day to day because they are too elaborate or expensive for an everyday meal. People typically hold fond memories of the food they eat on holidays. We remember the traditional foods our families ate year after year, recipes that may have been prepared only once a year for that special occasion. Those are the recipes that get passed down through the generations, and they are the ones we most looked forward to eating.

Historically, studying what families ate informs our understanding of the families' financial resources and how their daily lives were directly affected by events around them. In times of war, famine, or financial depression, food became scarce and diets looked radically different than the meals of more prosperous times. For example, in present-day America, meats we consider "acceptable" to eat include fish, beef, poultry, and pork. During war times, these meats were scarce and substitutions were made. In some cases vegetables replaced the protein found in meat, but in other instances, many animals now considered pets were used for meat. This idea is fully explored in chapter four.

Your family may have taken these hard-times food substitutions and incorporated them into its diet. In some cases these foods may have been seen as comfort foods or even reminders of how the family did with what they had. Others may have grown leery of foods that they had to make do with, and after the hard times ended, they never ate them again. Eating the same thing repeatedly can cure a person of ever eating a particular dish again. Lessons learned from hard times may have carried over to our families' everyday lives decades later. "Use it up, wear it out, make it do, or do without" is a motto some families lived by and applied to everything from clothing and material goods to food.

Food traditions can also reveal personality traits and personal preferences in an ancestor, which adds a depth of humanity. This knowledge can make the ancestor seem more relatable to future generations. Family members might want to know more about the life of a great-aunt after they taste her favorite cookie recipe. That same cookie recipe would be a great addition to a narrative about that great-aunt's life.

Your ancestors' diets may have been influenced by the health movements and attitudes of their times. These health fads may have been part of a religious belief or simply the social mores of the day that dictated what was healthy and what was not. While some of these fads faded away as quickly as they were introduced, other food reformers brought about foods and ideas that are still a part of our modern diet. Nineteenth-century diet reformer Sylvester Graham advocated that a vegetarian diet consisting largely of raw foods would increase health. The popular diet of his day, loaded with meat, potatoes and gravy, spicy foods, and alcohol, was one that he believed caused harm to those who partook of it. As an alternative, he developed a recipe for a cracker that was named for him and mass-marketed as the graham cracker, a food we still enjoy today, though not as he originally envisioned it. Physician John Harvey Kellogg popularized his ideas about vegetarianism at the turn of the twentieth century. (His views on vegetarianism are held by a contemporary religion, the Seventh-Day Adventists.) Kellogg's work in the field of nutrition, along with that of his brother Will Kellogg, changed the way Americans ate breakfast. What initially was a fad has become a staple of the current American diet—breakfast cereal.

A Celebration of Female Ancestors

The story of our food traditions is also largely the story of our female ancestors. Of course, men assisted in the gathering and preparation of food, but throughout history, this has been the work of women. Genealogy stresses the importance of gathering information that documents the lives of one's ancestors. Gathering evidence of their births, marriages, and deaths is an important aspect in re-creating a family history. But in some cases, especially with female ancestors, documentation can be scarce.

Female ancestors often didn't leave behind the same paper documentation as their male counterparts. While men left behind a paper trail rich with government and private-sector documents, women's lives were often relegated to the home. The material artifacts that they did leave behind are often considered unimportant and not worthy of archival efforts, which often means many women in our family trees are marked as *unknown*. Fortunately, the social history of food and family tradition can help fill in the gaps. Documenting the story of a female ancestor's life, including the work she contributed to her family, can help recount her story when other documents may not be available. The stories of women's lives must be told by more than the government or institutional records they left behind. Their history is best expressed through the traditions, stories, and artifacts that were part of their lives.

My family history includes stories of how my paternal great-grandmother, who was a professional cook, loved to feed people. She worked alongside her grandson, my dad, preparing meals in restaurants. Her mother, my great-great-grandmother, opened her kitchen to homeless people. My family history also includes memories of my maternal grandmother's kitchen, how the sink was low to the ground, giving the children no excuse to not help with the dishes while the women in the family talked and prepared meals. Her basement was full of shelf after shelf of home-canned fruits and vegetables. Thanksgiving meals, the kitchens, the smells of food—they all bring back memories of the family I have known and the family that I still share meals with. Although I may not continue to eat the foods prepared and presented by my grandmothers, great-grandmothers, and other female relatives, the stories of these women and the food that they prepared endure. I better understand their lives when I consider the everyday events of their lives—including feeding their families and helping others.

Your Family's Food Traditions

Close your eyes for a second and think about your own food memories. What comes to mind when you think about your family and your food traditions? Many people's memories revolve around special occasions like holidays and birthday celebrations. Families have their own unique ways of celebrating with food. Maybe your food memories revolve around the everyday foods your family ate. Perhaps those remembrances harken back to dishes that seemed to taste better when you were a child. Or maybe those memories include foods that you are happy never to eat again. When I think about what my family ate when I was younger, not only do the memories of the food fill my head but also the memories of who was there, who prepared the food, who helped, and the ways the food was served. My food-related memories are different than those of my children, even though we may eat the same dishes at every special occasion, because the memories are about more than the food. They are about the people we shared the food with.

For many, food is intrinsically connected to happy memories of family gatherings. I recently spoke at a meeting of an Italian genealogy society. I was struck by how joyfully and passionately the members described what their families prepared for Easter gatherings. Everyone was enjoying the mouth-watering descriptions of those foods remembered from long ago—antipasto plates with cheese and meats, lasagna made from old family recipes brought from Italy, and desserts piled high and drizzled with honey. But the memories contained more than just descriptions of meals. They contained memories of the people they shared the meal with. They remembered family members who had long passed away and family stories, and they were remembering their place in their own family history. Food has that effect. It not only feeds and nourishes our physical being, it also feeds our souls.

Your family food traditions might have been brought over from the old country, or maybe they are the result of a religious practice. Sometimes food traditions are intentionally handed down from generation to generation. And then there are food traditions with unknown origins, like the story I once heard of a woman who always cut off the end of her roast before placing it in the pan to cook. Pretty soon three generations of women were cutting off the end of the roast prior to cooking it. One day the grandmother was asked why she always cut the end off the roast. Her daughter was expecting an answer that would include tales from the family's history, the hardship they endured as immigrants, the lack of food, or something similar. The grandmother simply remarked that she had to cut off the roast's end because her roasting pan was too small. Maybe your food traditions started because of a new recipe your own mother tried that became a favorite with the family. Or your dinnertime staples may be recipes borrowed from someone else's family.

PRESERVING FOR FUTURE GENERATIONS

This book isn't just about the food traditions of your ancestors. It's also the story of the food you eat today. What you eat today may be influenced by what you grew up eating. In other cases, new traditions have replaced older ones. In either case, documenting and preserving what your family eats today is an important part of your family history archive. While this present-day record may not seem important to you now, it will be valuable to future generations. Family history should be not just the pursuit of the past but also the recording of the present for generations to come. One day in the not-too-distant future, your children or grandchildren will be wishing they had the recipe for their favorite special dish you made every holiday because it reminds them of you and their family history.

This book is a book of action. Use the information in it to learn more about your family food traditions and then find ways to preserve these traditions. There are numerous ways to pass on this information. Choose a style that reflects the uniqueness of your family.

Following are some suggestions to help you share the fruits of your food traditions research with your family. Whatever you decide to do, remember that what you preserve will allow future generations to better understand the distant ancestors you researched as well as your contemporary family.

SCRAPBOOK

A simple way to gather and share in a family's heritage is through a scrapbook that includes recipes and photos of your family preparing food in the kitchen, eating meals, and celebrating. Be sure to journal descriptions and explanations of the photos and recipes. Find inspiration for a format and embellishments in layout books that focus on heritage scrapbooks such as *Scrapbooking Your Family History* by the editors of *Creating Keepsakes Magazine*.

A digital scrapbook is an alternative to a traditional paper scrapbook. Just like genealogy, scrapbooking has come into the digital age. Digital scrapbooking uses images, graphics, and publishing software programs to manipulate and arrange photographs saved on your computer. You can use scans of old paper photos as well as new photos taken with a digital camera. After you finish your digital scrapbook, you can upload it to the internet, burn it to a CD or DVD, or print a hard copy either on your home printer or through a retailer that offers photo processing. A digital scrapbook is easier to share than a traditional paper scrapbook. You also have many options for archiving the material, such as using an automated backup system, uploading it to an online storage website, saving it to an external drive, or printing it out. Digital scrapbooks can also be less expensive to create than traditional scrapbooks.

Some traditional scrapbookers utilize a 12" x 12" format, whereas digital scrapbookers opt for an 8½" x 11" or smaller end result. Virtual embellishments, papers, and other scrapbook goodies are available to decorate digital pages just as you would a paper scrapbook album. Many different software programs and online sites, both fee-based and free, can assist you in creating a digital scrapbook to share with family members online or by printing it out. Some websites to check out are Scrap Girls <www.scrapgirls.com>, Creative Memories <www.creativememories. com>, Heritage Makers <www.heritagemakers.com>, and Scrapbook Flair <scrapbookflair.com>. Consider stopping in your local scrapbook store for ideas and assistance in creating a one-of-a-kind family keepsake.

A FAMILY HISTORY BOOK

The problem with most family history books is that they can seem dry and boring to those who don't enjoy genealogy. While loved by family historians, these books are very dense with pages of charts, dates, and numbering systems not understood by non-genealogists. These lists of name, dates, and locations can read like history textbooks. It's only when we add information and images about our ancestors' daily lives that these narratives come alive. Descendants want to read the story of their ancestors. They want to read about lives that they can relate to.

You may want to put together a short family history that is limited to only a generation or two and includes a few narratives of female ancestors. In addition to noting the dates and places important to their lives, add stories of their immediate family and their food traditions. You can also add interest by including photos of you re-creating an ancestor's recipe with step-by-step instructions. Put the history together using a word processing program or a genealogy software program, most of which let you easily create family history books with images, charts, and text.

After you create a family history book, you can share it with family members by burning it to a CD or DVD or by printing it with a basic binding. Most office supply stores and photocopy stores offer options for printing small booklets with your choice of binding—coil, comb, or another type of binding. Family history books don't need to be complex or costly.

If you are looking to create a book that will be professionally published, look for a printer that specializes in family history books. Do an online search for these publishing companies or find advertisements for them in genealogy magazines like *Family Tree Magazine*. Another printing option is to use a print-on-demand publisher who will print copies only when they are ordered by you or your family. This saves money over traditional publishing methods.

A FAMILY COOKBOOK

What better way to pass down family recipes and traditions than by creating a family cookbook that combines recipes used by earlier generations with the recipes of present-day family members? You can publish the book through a printing company that specializes in cookbooks, or you can create the book on your own and take it down to your local photocopy store to be printed. The benefit of using a specialized cookbook printing company is that they can assist you with adding sections, formatting recipes, adding recipes, uploading content online, and other considerations.

Family cookbooks don't need to be limited to recipes alone. Include the name and photos of a recipe's contributor, stories about the recipe, and other relevant family history photos. In a cookbook my cousin put together, each recipe included an introduction that identified the recipe's creator and explained the significance the recipe had to the family. She also included information about when it was served, especially if a dish was a holiday favorite. I also have a family cookbook that is based around a common ancestor on my maternal side. Each recipe includes a sentence that explains the relationship of the contributor to the common ancestor. This helps to better understand how other family members are related.

As you put together your cookbook, consider including pedigree charts or family group sheets. If the cookbook is presented in some type of three-ring binder, recipes can be added to the volume at a later date, allowing for additions as they are discovered or written down.

Not sure how to edit a cookbook? Look through your own collection or those found at a library or friend's home to get ideas about what you want your cookbook to look like. While not written with family cookbook editors in mind, the book *Will Write for Food* by Dianne Jacob does include a chapter on writing cookbooks. The book *Creating an Heirloom: Writing Your Family's Cookbook* by Wendy A. Boughner Whipple can also assist you in putting together a cookbook. Use e-mail, social networking sites, or word of mouth at holiday gatherings, reunions, or celebrations to start soliciting recipes from family members.

BLOG

Technology has provided us with great ways to share information with others. Many family historians use websites to post their research and their family trees. Another way to share family food history is by writing a blog. A blog, short for web log, is like a website but doesn't require any special internet programming knowledge. Anyone can create and maintain a blog. Within a matter of minutes, you can start a blog that shares family food memories, photos of family kitchens, dishes, linens, and other food-related items. Want to invite others to contribute to your blog? No problem; you can invite other relatives to be co-authors of your blog and share what they have found.

One benefit of a blog is that if the blog is made public, rather than private, search engines will include your blog in their hit results, making it easier for other family members to find you and share what they have as well.

Several blog programs provide everything you need to get started. Blog websites include Blogger <www.blogger.com>, WordPress <wordpress.com>, and TypePad <www.typepad.com>. You can get ideas for your blog by searching for other recipe, cookbook, genealogy, and family history blogs at Google Blog Search <google.com/ blogsearch>.

WIKIS

The internet is changing. What once was a collection of static websites has grown to include websites that encourage sharing and collaboration. *Web 2.0* is a term to describe this new internet generation that includes everything from social networking to cloud computing. Wikis are part of this next generation in websites. A wiki is a website that allows users to assist in the updating and posting of content. With wikis, unlike traditional websites, anyone can add information. Still not sure what a wiki is? One of the most popular wikis is the site Wikipedia <www.wikipedia.org>.

With a family wiki, you can create a website where family members can contribute recipes and images as well as comment on recipes, add family history information, and more. A wiki could be a wonderful family project that preserves family food traditions for generations of family members. The great thing about using a wiki is the format appeals to younger generations, so they are more likely to be interested in assisting with the project.

Various wiki websites exist that allow you to create a wiki for free, including Wikispaces <www.wikispaces.com>, Wikidot <www.wikidot.com>, and Zoho Wiki <www.zoho.com/wiki>. Check out the FamilySearch Research Wiki <wiki.familysearch.org> to get an idea of how a wiki might look. Specific cooking wikis include the Recipes Wiki <recipes.wikia.com>.

FAMILY FOOD HISTORY ARCHIVE

Catalog and preserve cookbooks, recipe cards, kitchen tools, linens, aprons, china, and silver to create a family food history archive. This archive can include photographs and written observations that document food traditions and food-related heirlooms and artifacts. Prepare a page for each item that includes the following information:

» the name of the item
» a physical description of the item (size, weight, color, markings, condition)
» where it came from (any story related to how it was obtained)
» provenance or the chain of ownership (who originally owned it, other owners, who owns it now)
» any special stories attached to the item (how it was/is used)
» where the item is located now (whose home it is stored in, how it is displayed)
» any condition concerns (holes, damage)
» photograph of the item

The final product can be a scrapbook (digital or physical), notebook, album, or electronic document sent to other family members. Include heirlooms that you own, but also interview family members to collect information on heirlooms they own. The final product will provide a nice

"A family history is not complete until it considers the time and place in which each individual lived. Our ancestors were affected by the events around them, just as people are now; their relationship to their environment is an important part of the family's story."—CARMEN J. FINLEY

history for family members as well as a practical guide to what family heir-looms exist along with descriptions should a disaster occur.

RESEARCH HISTORICAL PRICES OF FOOD

One way to make family history more interesting is by providing information that family members can relate to, and one concept everyone can relate to is the price of food. The other day, my children asked me how much gasoline cost when I was a teenager, and they were shocked at the difference in price between then and now. Help your family get a glimpse into their ancestors' lives by researching what food was available to your ancestors and the price of that food. You may be surprised to find that the prices of certain foods have remained almost the same for decades while others have changed dramatically. Use this information in a family history book, or cookbook, or on a blog or wiki. You can use these details to teach children about history and money by preparing a list of items with the prices as they were fifty or one hundred years ago and then taking them to a grocery store to record current food prices to make a comparison.

One place to find a history of grocery prices is the James Trager book, *The Food Chronology: A Food Lover's Compendium of Events and Anecdotes from Prehistory to the Present*. The website Food Timeline <www.foodtimeline.org/foodfaq5. html> offers various food history facts including historical food prices. You can also check out timeline websites that list historical information for your or someone else's birthdate including food prices. Time capsule websites include dMarie Time Capsule <dmarie.com/timecap>.

Also consider old newspapers. Advertisements for stores can be helpful for understanding what food was readily available and the prices as well as stores where your ancestor may have shopped. Newspapers for genealogical research can be found either at a repository like a library or archive or online. Some subscription websites with newspaper content include Godfrey Memorial Library <www.godfrey.org>, Ancestry.com <www.ancestry. com>, WorldVitalRecords <www.worldvitalrecords.com>, NewspaperArchive <www.newspaperarchive.com>, and GenealogyBank <www.genealogybank.com>. Be sure to search state, public, and university library online catalogs for newspapers available on microfilm.

A GENEALOGY DATABASE PROGRAM

Genealogy database software programs provide family historians many different ways to document and store their family history research. These software programs let you record facts and then include narrations or images to illustrate those facts, everything from a baptism to a marriage to military service. Find recipes from your family's kitchen or from their era and locale, and include that information as a "fact" for each female ancestor in your genealogy database program. Including this type of social history information can help fill in the gaps of that ancestor's life. This information will also be available if you choose to print out a report or book from your genealogy software program.

To find recipes from the past, consult cookbooks including those written by chefs and cooking school personnel, as well as those published by community groups, the government, and food and appliance manufacturers. You can find vintage cookbooks in libraries, archives, and digitized books as well as at online auctions websites, thrift stores, used bookstores (online and off), and antique stores. Chapter six is full of details to help you find old recipes.

Going From Here

This book is meant to be interactive. The first two parts of the book provide you the opportunity to learn more about food history and to reflect on your own family's food traditions. Use these sections to learn more about the historical role of food and its role in your family history.

Part three is a recipe journal in which you can collect family recipes and write your thoughts about important traditions. Be sure to document recipes from interviews with family members in this section. Use this book as a scrapbook of sorts. Refer to it for more ideas.

As you think of ways to preserve your family's food heritage, consider ways you can preserve your family's current traditions. Vow today to record not only the past but also the present. Your lifetime will be something that your grandchildren and their children will be curious about. You can record the present the same way you record the past. Apply the ideas in this chapter to your own life. You may find it's easier to record the present as you write down recipes, recall celebrations, and photograph your own kitchen necessities.

While genealogy has long been the pursuit of names and dates, the true study of a family's history involves learning more about the lives your ancestors lived. Part of learning more about them is incorporating the "everyday" into the story of their lives. Family history has more meaning for descendants when they can liken their ancestors' lives to their own. And in a rapidly changing world, one thing stays constant: families gathering around the table to share a meal.

NOTES

» [1] Katherine Scott Sturdevant, *Bringing Your Family History to Life Through Social History* (Cincinnati: Betterway Books, 2000), 6.

CHAPTER

2

They Brought Their Food With Them

24

The traveler indeed will find in China good eating of every sort—except chop suey. —THE MIXER AND SERVER, 1912

If you live in America, you likely live near some standard ethnic restaurants—that is Mexican, Chinese, or Italian. The truth is most of the dishes served in these restaurants originated in America, and while they may have been inspired by or first created by immigrants, many of the dishes are unknown in the native countries. Unless you live in a major city or near a large immigrant population, you're unlikely to encounter absolutely authentic ethnic food simply because many of the necessary ingredients are hard to come by here in America. Your immigrant ancestors would have experienced the same difficulties when they arrived in this country, whether they emigrated two hundred years ago or thirty years ago. This chapter looks at the true origins of ethnic food in America and includes stories of actual immigrants who brought food traditions with them.

From Chop Suey to Matzo Balls

Immigrant communities cook the food they grew up with or are accustomed to. They look for ingredients that they know or find as passable substitutes. Ethnic markets spring up to provide the community with the taste of home that they long for. But that is not the case in the ethnic restaurants that serve a wider community of people outside of the immigrant community. This population is not familiar with the look or smell of the cuisine. In most ethnic restaurant settings, whether Mexican or Chinese, the food served is going to appeal to local taste palates and not necessarily reflect the food of the country.

ITALIAN

If you are not from an Italian background, the mention of Italian food may conjure up images of red checkered tablecloths and bottles of wine, maybe even plastic grapes hanging from faux arbors. But the food we think of as Italian is quite different from the food that is truly Italian. Sure, they still eat lasagna and pizza, but the so-called Italian foods non-Italians eat tend to be heavy with cheese and tomato sauce, whereas food in Italy is healthier and much more diverse because it takes advantage of fresh vegetables, seafood, and olive oil.

While there were some Italian immigrants to American during the colonial period, between 1890 and 1924 Italians immigrated to America in droves for economic reasons.[1] The immigrants settled in ethnic enclaves, and little Italys starting popping up in large urban centers.[2] While Italian food is now one of the more popular cuisines in America, it was not always so widely accepted. Assimilation into American culture was seen as vital in the early twentieth century, and sticking to ethnic customs, even food traditions, was seen as detrimental. In 1920, a New York social worker wrote of one of her charges, "Not assimilated yet—still eating pasta."[3]

Pizza is one of the most popular Italian dishes in America today. Italian immigrants to America were making pizzas in bakeries at the close of the nineteenth century. The first pizzeria in the United States was Lombardi's in New York City, which opened in 1905. Gennaro Lombardi was making pizza in a bakery in America as early as 1897, but didn't open his own pizza restaurant until eight years later. Originally from Naples, Lombardi took his knowledge of Italian pizza making and adapted it to his new homeland, substituting ingredients and cooking methods available in the United States. At the turn of the twentieth century, Italian food in American was being made by Italians for Italians, but after the Great Depression, non-Italian Americans were eating Italian food and pizza in Italian restaurants. However, pizza didn't start to gain popularity until after World War II. Returning soldiers had enjoyed pizza in Italy and sought out the dish after they returned home. As non-Italian Americans embraced pizza, it evolved from the tomato pie that was served in Italy to having more cheese and thicker crust. Chicago deep-dish pizza was created in 1943.

CHINESE

To understand the Chinese food eaten in restaurants all over the United States, we need to first understand the Chinese immigrant population and its history in the United States. Chinese immigrants started coming to the United States in the nineteenth century. Shortly thereafter, immigration laws were changed to exclude Chinese immigrants. The Chinese Exclusion Act (1882) put a stop to Chinese immigration and restricted the ability of those who were already here from re-entering after a visit to China. The act was not repealed until 1943. This legislation greatly affected Chinese men who were already in the United States. They typically came without their wives and families, and once here it was almost impossible for their wives to join them. Without wives in the home, many Chinese men were required to take on household duties traditionally done by women, including laundry and cooking.

Many Chinese found work building the railroad across the nation. Their white employers viewed Chinese workers as disposable, so the Chinese were often given the most dangerous assignments. They also took mining jobs and were often hated and persecuted by white miners who viewed the immigrants as competition. After the railroad was completed, the Chinese took jobs that were entrepreneurial in nature, and many owned laundries and restaurants.

In nineteenth-century America, there was great prejudice against the Chinese, and that prejudice extended to food. Most white Americans in the nineteenth century found Chinese food odd, both in look and smell. They told stories of Chinese people eating rats, dogs, and cats.

Chinese staples such as fortune cookies and chop suey are on every Chinese restaurant menu in America, but as author Jennifer Lee points out, these dishes aren't real Chinese food.[4] So if these dishes didn't come from China, where did they come from?

The actual origins of chop suey are hard to track down. One explanation is that a Chinese cook trying to feed miners simply added a little bit of this and that. No matter the origin, chop suey became so popular in the United States that it was a shock when early twentieth-century American tourists traveled to China and discovered no one there knew of the dish. In the trade journal *The Mixer and Server* from 1912, a tourist wrote, "Chop Suey Hoax Exposed: Sold in the United States as China's National Dish, But Orientals Have Never Heard Of It." The article went on to say that the ingredients found in chop suey weren't even eaten by the Chinese. In America, the dish was made with beef, but the tourist wrote, "A Chinaman of China very rarely tastes beef, for not only is the religious influence of the Buddhists against the eating of any beast of burden, but there is not enough grazing land in the empire to make it possible for beef to be raised for consumptions."[5]

JEWISH

Delicatessen is from a German word that means "delicacies." While we associate delicatessens or delis with the Jewish culture, the first delis in America were owned by Germans and sold foods like sausages, sauerkraut, meatloaf, frankfurters, liverwurst, and pretzels. Germans were one of the largest immigrant groups coming to America after the American Civil War, and a good percentage of them were Jewish.[6]

Jewish entrepreneurs started selling foods from pushcarts to other immigrants. These food pushcart businesses were a family effort with the wife making the food in the family apartment and the husband selling it later in the day. Because the food was sold to workers, it had to be portable and preserved so as not to spoil. Popular pushcart foods included knishes, black breads, ryes, bagels, pickled herring, cold meats, and pickles. Over time, the pushcarts disappeared and delis started springing up.[7] Jewish delis provide patrons with a mix of cured meats, fish, and sandwiches.

By 1931, there were 1,550 kosher delicatessen stores in the New York City boroughs.[8] Due to various factors including the rise of full-service grocery stores and migrations from cities to suburbs, the Jewish deli in New York City has almost gone the way of the dinosaur. According to author David Sax, fewer than fifty are left in the boroughs.

MEXICAN

For some areas of the United States, Mexican food was a part of the region's early history. The cuisines of California, Arizona, Texas, and New Mexico have all been influenced by the first settlers to these regions—the Spanish. The food eaten by these earlier settlers was very different from the Mexican food Americans eat today. It was even different from the food eaten by people in modern-day Mexico. For example, a standard midmorning repast for Mexican cowboys in 1769 California would have included chorizo y frijoles, tortillas, queso, vino tinto, burritos de carne con chile, frijoles refritors, and café. A noonday dinner might include puchero-caldo, carne, verduras (boiled pot with broth, meat, and vegetables), ensalada de verdolagas (pigweed salad), tortillas, and vine tinto or café.[9]

At the turn of the twentieth century, most "Mexican" food served in California used beef as a main ingredient. Dishes also included olives, raisins, and grapes as part of fillings for enchiladas and chiles rellenos, for example, because these foods were readily available in the region, and the "meals were always accompanied by wine."[10]

Salsa is the Spanish word for *sauce*. This dish can be made in a variety of ways, though most Americans are used to a red, tomato-based version. Salsa became popular with Americans, especially in the Southwest, after the 1940s. The first bottled salsas began appearing on store shelves during this time, making access to salsa easier.[11] Today salsa can be found in non-Mexican restaurants (in some areas of the country McDonalds has salsa packets available alongside ketchup packets), grocery stores stock wide varieties of salsa, and stores catering to "chile heads" sell hot sauces that make jalapenos taste like a dessert.

28

THE IMMIGRANTS' EXPERIENCE

Journeying to a foreign country takes faith. There are challenges to starting a new life in a place where the language is foreign, the people are different, and everything is unknown, including the food. Many immigrants arrived in America with very little, but they did bring their knowledge of the recipes and foods of their homeland. In some families, those food traditions are carefully passed down and taught to each generation of women.

However, over time this knowledge may become diluted as descendants Americanize recipes and lose a taste for ingredients that are staples in the homeland but a rarity in America. Sometimes recipes were changed because the traditional ingredients weren't available in the immigrants' new country. Through travels and interviews with family members and

Italian cooks, author Laura Schenone discovered her family's ravioli recipe uses Philadelphia Cream Cheese in the filling because it was a close substitute for the cheese her family used back in Italy. She chronicles her journey in pursuit of her family's ravioli recipe in *The Lost Ravioli Recipes of Hoboken: A Search for Food and Family*.

In her book, *97 Orchard: An Edible History of Five Immigrant Families in One New York Tenement*, Jane Ziegelman describes German krauthobblers who went door to door slicing cabbage for sauerkraut at the turn of the twentieth century.[12] These krauthobblers likely provided continuity between the way sauerkraut was made in Germany and the borough they served. But as technology made krauthobblers obsolete, one connection to the old country was lost, which could make it more difficult to follow the traditional recipes and methods.

A CONTEMPORARY IMMIGRANT

Recent immigrants can often give us the best perspective on how foodways change when moving from one country to another. Their diets often incorporate the foods they know from their homeland as well as those of their newly adopted country.

In the 1980s, Teresa Bettancourt Philibert immigrated to the United States from the island country of São Jorge in the Azores when she was a teenager. The language and culture were entirely new to her, as was the food. In São Jorge, Teresa's family had produced most of the food they ate through gardening, raising animals, and fishing. They purchased very few food items from a small, nearby store. She was used to fresh, organic foods grown right in her yard. She immediately noticed a difference in the taste of food in the United States. "Even the sugar here tastes different," Teresa says.

The following cookie recipe is a specialty of São Jorge. It's made for holidays, festivals, and special occasions.

....

ESPÉCIES (SPECIALTY OF SÃO JORGE, AZORES)
White dough:
  1 kg all-purpose flour
  125 g of butter
  2 eggs
  1 pinch of salt
  1 tablespoon of lard
  Cold water

Place all the ingredients except water in the food processor. With the food processor running, slowly add water until the dough forms a ball. Set aside.

Filling:
  1 kg of sugar
  ½ kg of toasted bread flour
  Zest of 3 lemons
  50 g of cinnamon
  50 g of anise
  1 liter of water
  4 tablespoons of butter
  White pepper to taste

Place all the ingredients minus the flour and butter in a heavy stockpot, bring to boil, and boil the mix for about 10 minutes stirring it occasionally. Remove from heat, add the butter, mix, and then add the flour, and mix again. Set aside and let cool.

To assemble the cookies, divide the white dough into four to six pieces. Roll out the dough with a rolling pin to $\frac{1}{16}$ inch thickness, and then cut into strips 3 inches wide and 6 inches long. Make 5 to 6 diagonal cuts on one side of the dough with a pastry crimper. To make the center, fill a pastry bag fitted with a wide tip with the filling, and pipe the filling onto the length of the dough. Fold over the dough so the side with the diagonal cuts is facing up. Crimp the edges, and form them into a horseshoe shape that connects at the tips.

Bake at 350°F on a baking sheet until lightly golden. Set aside and let cool.

FOOD AS A NECESSITY

In her e-book *Value Meals on the Volga*, genealogist Anna Dalhaimer Bartkowski records her family history, food traditions, and the recipes of her Russian immigrant grandmother who came from the German-Russian town of Mariental. According to Bartkowski, her grandparents "did not dine, they ate."[13] Even in the United States, vegetables and meats were considered a treat on their dinner table. Before refrigeration and high-speed shipping methods, fresh produce was only available in season, and even then it was only what could be grown locally. Meat was expensive and hard to keep fresh for more than a day. As a result, dairy, eggs, and grains constituted a large part of our ancestors' diets before the nineteenth century. Anna records a number of the recipes her grandmother's family used, including one she and her sister called "the stuff in the brown pan" because they had trouble pronouncing the name.

....

SOUR CREAM MAULDASHA A.K.A. RA MAULTASCHEN

(pronounced sour cream mull da sha or ra mull da sha)

Ingredients:

  3 cups flour

  1 tablespoon salt

  ½ tablespoon sugar

  1 teaspoon baking powder

  2 eggs

  1½ cups water

  3 tablespoons butter

  4 cups milk

  8 oz. sour cream

Preheat oven to 450 ° F. Mix flour, salt, sugar, baking powder, and eggs in large bowl. Add 1½ cups of water. Mix together until all ingredients form dough. Knead the dough until smooth.

Add flour if necessary to make a stiff but malleable dough. Use rolling pin to spread out thinly, approximately ¼ inch thick, on a floured board.

Set 13" x 9" x 2" pan with 3 tablespoons of butter in it over a burner. Heat butter on low until melted. Warm 4 cups milk on low heat on stovetop and set aside.

Spread sour cream over the flattened dough just like you would spread frosting on a cake. Cut the dough with a sharp knife into square or rectangular pieces. Roll up each piece lengthwise into a circular tube, like a Swiss cake roll. Set each tube into the pan with the melted butter. Arrange in pan as it best fits. Pour warm milk over rolls.

Bake in 450°F oven for approximately 30 minutes. Lower oven temperature after milk boils. Meal serves family of four for two meals. Leftovers can be cut up and reheated in frying pan or microwave.[14]

Because the United States is such a melting pot of cultures, odds are good that your everyday diet has been shaped in some way by immigrants and ethnic traditions. While some of us may have ethnic food that is a part of our everyday lives, those of us who are more removed generationally from our immigrant ancestors may not be as lucky. How can you learn more about your ethnic food traditions? Reading other people's stories of their food traditions can be a start. Consider such compilations as *Pilaf, Pozole, and Pad Thai: American Women and Ethnic Food* by Sherrie A. Innes and *Storied Dishes: What Our Family Recipes Tell Us About Who We Are and Where We've Been* by Linda Murray Burzok.

Aside from searching out ethnic cookbooks, try looking for older community cookbooks from your ancestor's home to get a sense of what may have been cooking on your ancestor's stove. Also consider regional history books and the biographical writings of those who share your ancestor's cultural and ethnic background.

NOTES

» [1] John P. Colletta, *Finding Italian Roots: The Complete Guide for Americans* (Baltimore: Genealogical Publishing Co., 1993), 16.

» [2] Ibid., 17.

» [3] Stewart Lee Allen, *In the Devil's Garden: A Sinful History of Forbidden Food* (New York: Ballantine Books, 2002), 103.

» [4] Jennifer Lee, *The Fortune Cookie Chronicles: Adventures in the World of Chinese Food* (New York: Twelve, 2008), 34.

» [5] Ibid., 34.

» [6] David Sax, *Save the Deli: In Search of Perfect Pastrami, Crusty Rye, and the Heart of Jewish Delicatessen* (Boston: Houghton Mifflin Harcourt, 2009), 23.

» [7] Ibid., 24.

» [8] Ibid., 27.

» [9] Ana Bégué Packman, *Early California Hospitality: The Cookery Customs of Spanish California, With Authentic Recipes and Menus of the Period* (Glendale, Calif: The Arthur H. Clark Co., 1938), 45.

» [10] Charles Perry, "Piedad Yorba," *Gastronomica* 10 (Summer 2010): 53.

» [11] Andrew F. Smith, ed., *The Oxford Companion to American Food and Drink* (Oxford: Oxford University Press, 2007), 517.

» [12] Jane Ziegelman, *97 Orchard: An Edible History of Five Immigrant Families in One New York Tenement* (New York: HarperCollins, 2010), xiii.

» [13] Anna Dalhaimer Bartkowski, *Value Meals on the Volga: Sharing Our Heritage With New Generations* (Fargo, North Dakota: Germans From Russian Heritage Collection, 2006), 5.

» [14] Ibid., 31.

CHAPTER 3

Oysters, Peacocks, and Green Jell-O

34

"...Peacock which, tho', beautifully plumaged,
is tough, hard, stringy, and untasted, and even indelicious..."
—AMELIA SIMMONS, 1798

I 'll never forget my first lesson in regional food differences. I was about eleven years old and visiting a cousin out of state. One night I volunteered to help prepare dinner and was told we were having "burros." Panic raced through my mind as I imagined eating a small, horse-like creature. It didn't seem like something normal people ate. I knew I would have to eat some because I was taught to always be polite and to try every food put in front of me. My stomach churned at the thought of the upcoming meal. My anxiety built for about thirty minutes until I realized that when my relatives said "burros," they weren't referring to the animal but to a burrito, a food I was very familiar with living in Southern California.

Anyone who has traveled out of his region knows that food differences exist. What is a very familiar food for me in California may be nonexistent as you travel east. Even areas within a region may have access to foods that are different from foods found in a city only an hour away. Foods I have dined on in the southern states, like fried okra and collard greens for example, are harder to come by when I come home to the West.

Mark Kurlansky, editor of *The Food of a Younger Land,* mentions that as he traveled, he found that "being raised in New England and New York, I was struck by the differences in how people ate in other parts of the country—how breakfasts get bigger as you traveled west and hamburgers became increasingly adorned until by California they were virtually a salad sandwich."[1]

Most tourists or travelers encounter regional foods at local non-chain restaurants. A few examples include Fry Sauce in Utah; the Horseshoe Sandwich in Springfield, Illinois; West Indies Salad in Birmingham, Alabama; the Hot Brown in Louisville, Kentucky; Cincinnati-style chili in Cincinnati, Ohio; the Juicy Lucy in South Minneapolis; and the Philadelphia Cheesesteak in Philadelphia. Many times, these regional foods may be the invention of a local chef who was meeting a need. The new dish then became so popular that it started a trend in the city or area, and other restaurants began offering a similar dish. The Hot Brown, a toasted, open-faced sandwich stacked with slices of turkey, ham, bacon, and sliced tomato and covered with cheese sauce and Parmesan cheese, was invented by Fred K. Schmidt, a chef at the Brown Hotel, who created it to serve to hungry guests who attended the nightly dinner-dances at the hotel.

Not so long ago many of the regional food differences existed because of lack of refrigeration, landscape, growing seasons, transportation, availability, and immigrant communities. In today's world, food differences may be more of a product of regionalism and culture. This chapter explores the foodways—that is the cultural, economic, and social practices surrounding food—of the various regions of the United States to help you better understand what your ancestors might have eaten. You'll also see how the foodways of the past continue to influence present-day diets. See the bibliography for books on regional cuisines for additional ideas about how your family ate.

FOODWAYS IN THE NORTHEAST

The Northeast has food traditions stretching back to the very beginnings of the nation. New England states are primarily associated with fresh seafood.

Early settlers quickly established a fishing industry to harvest food from the Atlantic Ocean. Other New England staples include johnnycakes, a type of flat cornbread, and baked beans. While the seafood connection is obvious, how did Boston come to be known as Bean Town? The answer is found in colonial times.

While colonial Americans brought their British food customs with them to America, baked beans is most likely not one of them. Colonists saw that the American Indians prepared beans with maple sugar and bear fat, and the dish became very popular with the colonists.

The first recorded recipe for baked beans appears in Lydia Maria Francis Child's 1829 work, *The American Frugal Housewife dedicated to those who are not ashamed of economy*. The term *Boston baked beans* was first coined in the midnineteenth century.[2]

The popularity of baked beans might be summed up in a story found in the *History of Brooklyn, Susquehanna Co., Penn'a: Its Homes and Its People* (1889), which relates that beans were popular among earlier settlers because "they were wholesome and nutritious, easily produced and gave quick returns."[3]

36

In the *History of the Eleventh Regiment, Rhode Island Volunteers, in the war of the rebellion*, the author comments that once the men had settled into the idea that they were going to be involved in the Civil War for a while, they decided to improve their cookhouses. "Coming from Yankee land they were bound to gratify their desire for baked beans."[4] Bricks were scavenged from dilapidated houses, and beans and bacon were supplied by Uncle Sam.

Though once truly baked in crocks, baked beans are now mostly stewed in a sauce, and there are many canned varieties available that only need to be heated, not cooked. Heinz first tested canned baked beans in Britain in 1905 and eventually sold more cans in Britain than in the United States. In a December 21, 1936, *Life* magazine advertisement, Heinz boasted that they had reverently studied the New England recipes so they would know the correct amounts of molasses, pork, and brown sugar to use. The company went on to boast that Bostonians thanked them for these canned beans and noted how they were shipping the beans to Boston, the home of the Boston-style bean.

Pennsylvania, like other states, was influenced by the immigrant and religious groups that settled there. Pennsylvania Dutch greatly influenced the foodways of the Keystone State. The Pennsylvania Dutch are immigrants and descendants of immigrants from southwestern Germany and Switzerland. The term *Dutch* should not be confused with people from the Netherlands. Those who are Pennsylvania Dutch are not from just one religion, but include Lutherans, Amish, and Mennonites. These immigrants settled in Pennsylvania in the seventeenth and eighteenth centuries. One of their dishes, scrapple, is all but unknown to many people living outside the area.

Scrapple is a spiced pork sausage that contains pork scraps, flour, cornmeal, and spices. This mixture is formed into a congealed loaf, and then slices are taken from the loaf and pan-fried. Scrapple can also be deep-fried or broiled. Often served with condiments like maple syrup, ketchup, jelly, and apple butter, scrapple is most commonly served at breakfast but can also be served at other times.

THANKSGIVING

School children learn the story of the Pilgrims and Indians sharing the first Thanksgiving in New England. While many of the details of that story are probably false, the idea behind it gave us the holiday we know today. Though the first Thanksgiving was a three-day event celebrated in 1621, Thanksgiving was not recognized as a federal holiday until 1863. Prior to that, Thanksgiving was an event celebrated mostly in New England, and the date of the celebration differed from state to state.

Sarah Josepha Buell Hale (1788-1879), an American writer and editor of one of the first women's magazines (*Godey's Lady's Book*), campaigned for forty years among mayors, governors, and five presidents in an effort to have Thanksgiving declared a national holiday. Although virtually unknown today, Hale was responsible for many forward-thinking ideas such as public playgrounds for children and daycare for working mothers. Today she is probably best known as the author of the nursery rhyme "Mary Had a Little Lamb."

In 1827, she wrote that far too few national holidays existed and that Thanksgiving should be a national holiday like the Fourth of July. Her vision was to set aside a day both to give thanks for all that we have and to remember the poor. In an editorial she wrote in *Godey's Lady's Book*, Hale said, "Let the people of all states and territories sit down together to the 'feast of fat things,' and drink, in the sweet draught of joy and gratitude to the Divine giver of all blessings, the pledge of renewed love to the Union, and to each other, and peace and good-will to all men."

In 1863, President Abraham Lincoln finally granted Hale's wish and set aside the last Thursday in November as a national day of thanksgiving. His Thanksgiving Proclamation was issued just four months prior to the Gettysburg Address.

The Thanksgiving meal has evolved over time. Food served at the first Thanksgiving, and many after that, would have been whatever was local, including corn, fish, and animals that could have been procured through hunting, like fowl or deer. However, it wasn't too long before the Thanksgiving we are all familiar with came into being. Amelia Simmons's cookbook, published in 1796, includes several traditional Thanksgiving dishes or dishes that modern Americans would recognize, including butter gravy, cranberry sauce, relish tray, boiled onions, boiled cabbage, butter biscuits, pumpkin pie, Indian pudding, flavored whipped cream, and cookies.[5]

Of course Thanksgiving menus reflect the place and who is serving the food. Consider the differences in the two following Thanksgiving menus. The first, served on the Plains in 1868, features foods that were mostly hunted and gathered, while the menu from the Maison Tortoni restaurant reflects foods that those living in the latter nineteenth century would expect at a fine restaurant, including favorites like oysters and turtle soup.

Journalist DeBenneville Randolph Keim accompanied General Philip Sheridan during the Indian Wars. Keim's writing gives a sense of an 1868 Thanksgiving menu on the Oklahoma plains. It features a great amount of meat, something the soldiers could have hunted where they were camped. The menu according to Keim:

38

Soup—Wild Turkey
Boiled—Wild Turkey, Buffalo Tongue
Roast—Buffalo Hump, Wild Turkey, Saddle of Venison, Red Deer, Common Deer, Antelope, Rabbit
Entrees—Rabbit Pies, Wings of Grouse, Turkey Giblets
Vegetables (imported)—Canned Tomatoes, Lima Beans, Desiccated Potatoes
Bread—Hard Tack, plain and toasted, Army Biscuits
Dessert (imported)—Rice Pudding, Pies, and Tarts
Wines and Liquors—Chamapgne [sic], "Pinetop Wiskey [sic]," Ale.[6]

In 1897, the Maison Tortoni restaurant in Seattle, Washington, featured this Thanksgiving menu:

Chicken Salad
Boned Turkey
Eastern Oysters on Half-Shell
Olives

Celery

Green Turtle Soup a la Maryland

Mountain Trout au Gratin

Pommes Parisienne (French Potatoes)

Frogs a la Poulette

Asparagus au Branch

Omelette Soufflé au Maraschino

Vanilla Ice Cream

Assorted Fruits

Roquefort Cheese

Camembert Cheese

Café Noir with Cognac[7]

NEW YORK CITY

Most people think of New York City as a melting pot of foods from all over the world. Today the city's more than 23,000 restaurants attest to New York being the place to try new foods and innovative creations by world-class chefs.[8]

New York City was home to some of the busiest immigration ports in the country—Castle Garden in the mid-nineteenth century and Ellis Island, which opened in 1892. The city reflects this diverse culinary heritage with a history of ethnic restaurants and food carts that pepper the city. German immigrants brought New York City its first ethnic cuisine in 1840.[9] Today ethnic cuisines from throughout the world—including Korean, Indian, Filipino, Czech, Puerto Rican, Jamaican, Russian, and others—can be found in the five boroughs alongside ethnic restaurants more familiar to the rest of the United States like Mexican, Italian, and Chinese.

While New York City's food history is a diverse one, it was not always so. In the days of the earliest colonists, when the area was still named New Amsterdam, colonists ate diets typical to other settlers of the New World—dried beans, salted meats, seafood, cheese, beer, and game.[10] Their diets changed with the times and included foods acquired through trade. Restaurants opening in the early nineteenth century included oyster houses and some restaurants familiar to modern-day diners including Delmonico's.

MIDWEST

Often called "the breadbasket of America," the Midwest is a region associated with American food. It is here that beef, pork, grains, and dairy are the norm. The flat, fertile soil provided ample grazing areas for cows and made it easy to raise large crops of corn and wheat. The first white settlers of the area were from New York, New Jersey, and Pennsylvania.[11] Early settlers in this agrarian society ate foods like bread, meats, and potatoes.

British and German immigrants then began settling in the Midwest. Northern Europeans settled in the Upper Midwest and Great Lakes region, while Irish and Eastern Europeans migrated to the urban centers.[12] German settlers brought their food traditions of pork, sausages, sauerkraut, and root vegetables. They also carried on their traditional methods of making cheese and crafting beers, and these practices can be seen in this region to this day.[13] The famous Sheboygan bratwurst, a grilled ground-pork sausage served on a hard roll with butter and fried onions, is an example of the German food heritage found in the area.

Amish and Mennonite communities in Ohio and Indiana brought with them foods heavy in carbohydrates and meats. They are known for their "homemade noodles, chicken and dumplings, mashed potatoes, cabbage, homemade pickles and jams … and pies."[14]

THE SOUTH

Most people think of eating fried foods and barbecue when they think of the South in the United States. Comfort foods like fried chicken and mashed potatoes and gravy along with regional vegetables such as greens and okra come to mind. But the South is a large region with a great diversity of foods. Just look at the countless styles of barbecue that are available. Each region or city seems to have its own style of sauce or rub.

Pigs have long been a staple of Southern cooking, including the use of smoked pork products like bacon and ham and barbecued pork. Originally pigs were left to run wild in the South and were hunted; later they were kept on farms.

Vegetables like corn, green beans, sweet potatoes, onions, cucumbers, and butter beans grew well in the South because of the long growing season, and vegetables and side dishes are still popular in Southern cooking. Some plants like tomatoes and eggplants were grown in the South before they were grown anywhere else in the United States.[15] Vegetables, a large part of Southern meals, include fried or cooked vegetables as well as vegetables preserved through relishes and pickling.

AFRICAN-AMERICAN INFLUENCES

Women who were enslaved during America's early history had an impact on Southern cooking, both during slavery and long after it was abolished.

Using scraps, less-desirable parts of animals, and their own gardens, these women cooked food for their families and for the white families they served. Later, after the abolishment of slavery, these women continued to cook for their own families and in the homes of white families where they worked.

African slaves brought with them foods that are now considered staples of Southern cooking, including rice, yams, black-eyed peas, okra, mustard greens, sweet potatoes, peanuts, and other vegetables. As slaves, they grew this produce in their private gardens.[16]

The term *greens* refers to the leafy tops of some vegetables and leaf vegetables, including beet tops, turnip tops, spinach, collard, and mustard greens. Slaves brought the tradition of eating greens with them from Africa (greens are also popular in Brazil and Portugal). Greens were cooked in water with bacon or ham hocks. The end result produces not only the cooked greens but also "pot likker." Pot likker becomes part of the served dish and is soaked up with cornbread. The benefit of eating the pot likker along with the greens is that it contained the vitamins and minerals leached out during the cooking process.[17]

The recipes cooked by African-American women for white families and their own were initially passed down orally; however there were early African-American cooks who did write down these recipes. One example is Abby Fisher, who was a slave and later a successful businesswoman. In her cookbook, *What Mrs. Fisher Knows About Old Southern Cooking, Soups, Pickles, Preserves, Etc.* (1881), she provides recipes for some of the food that we associate with Southern food today, such as plantation corn bread or hoe cake, fried chicken, ochra [sic], gumbo, and sweet potato pie.

As African-Americans started moving to the north in the twentieth century, the soul food movement was born. What became known as soul food in the late 1960s was influenced by foods born out of slavery, sharecropping, and poverty. According to James C. McCann in his book *Stirring the Pot: A History of African Cuisine*, soul food has two characteristics: The first is that many of the ingredients have an African origin such as collard greens, okra, watermelon, and black-eyed peas. The second is the food has regional variation—ingredients and recipes differ all over the South.[18]

CREOLE AND CAJUN

Louisiana has a rich history that includes Creole and Cajun peoples. Creoles are the descendants of colonial French, Haitian, and Spanish settlers in Louisiana. Cajuns are an ethnic group descended from exiled Acadians (from whence the word *Cajun* comes), who left Canada after the French and Indian War. The diets in the bayous are unique to the region and influenced by French traditions and the food readily available, including alligator, shrimp, crab, crawfish, lobsters, and oysters. Food like gumbo (a stew with meat or seafood), cracklins (deep-fried pig skin), boudin (a sausage), étouffée (a thick stew of shellfish served over rice), and jambalaya (a rice-based dish with meats, vegetables, and spices similar to paella) are staples in the cuisine of this region.

The first published jambalaya recipe can be found in the 1881 African-American cookbook *What Mrs. Fisher Knows About Old Southern Cooking, Soups, Pickles, Preserves, Etc*. This recipe does not contain all of the ingredients normally associate with jambalaya.

....

JUMBERLIE—A CREOLE DISH

Take one chicken and cut it up, separating every joint, and adding to it one pint of cleanly-washed rice. Take about half a dozen large tomatoes, scalding them well and taking the skins off with a knife. Cut them in small pieces and put them with the chicken in a pot or large porcelain saucepan. Then cut in small pieces two large pieces of sweet ham and add it to the rest, seasoning high with pepper and salt. It will cook in twenty-five minutes. Do not put any water on it.[19]

French isn't the only influence in this area. Dishes here also have influences from the Spanish, Portuguese, Italians, Greeks, American Indians, and African-Americans.

Texas and the Southwest

The foods of the Southwest reflect the early history of the area—settled by American Indians and later Spanish explorers and Mexican inhabitants. Foods such as corn, beans, and chili peppers were the basis of food from this region, but then the food was transformed by the immigrant populations who settled here. Corn was transformed into masa for tamales and tortillas, and, when treated with lye, made hominy for pozole (a Mexican soup made with hominy, pork, and red chile). Chili peppers were used for everything from stuffing to sauces.

In 1823, Anglo residents started moving into what is now Texas with land grants from the Mexican government. The later discovery of gold brought additional waves of Americans and Europeans to this region.[20] German immigrants to Texas brought sausages and potatoes with them. As more Anglos came to the area, beef, pork, and potatoes were added to the foods, and eventually new chili peppers were developed that were milder to appeal to the tastes of non-Hispanics.[21] As Americans from the southern states started to migrate to Texas, they brought bacon, ham, cornbread, and biscuits.

The influx of Anglo and Southern foods helped to influence Tex-Mex cuisine. One example of this cuisine is chili con carne, a mixture of beef and red chile.[22] Other southwestern cuisines include such dishes as barbecued beef brisket, Navajo tacos (an open-faced taco on Navajo fry bread topped with refried beans, lettuce, tomatoes, cheese, avocado, sour cream, and salsa), son-of-a-gun stew (a stew made from beef organ meat), machaca (made with beef or pork and served with eggs or in a burrito, taco, or flauta) and cheese crisps (flour tortillas baked with cheese).[23]

CALIFORNIA

California cuisine is influenced by its long growing season and its produce-friendly climate, which is suitable to everything from citrus to berries to avocados. It also has heavy Mexican and Spanish influences because they were the original settlers of the area. California is also home to major Pacific Ocean ports that welcomed almost all of the Asian immigrants, and their influence is seen as well.

Printed in California in 1898, *El Cocinero Español* by Encarnación Pinedo was the first Spanish cookbook published in the United States. Some of the recipes documented are still staples in California cuisine today.

PACIFIC NORTHWEST

Pioneers to the Pacific Northwest of the United States had to make do with what they had. Like pioneers to any region, supplies were few and far between, and in many cases even the local merchants, when there were merchants, had shortages. According to author Jacqueline B. Williams in *The Way We Ate: Pacific Northwest Cooking, 1843-1900*, water had to be hauled, cooking outdoors or in a fireplace substituted for a stove, and basic ingredients like flour, sugar, and coffee were often in short supply. She writes that substitutions like pie filling made with beans and sheep sorrel instead of fruit were just one of the ways those early pioneers made do with what they had.[24]

Today we associate this region with salmon, and the same was true for early settlers. Large amounts of fish and wild game were available to them, though not all game was considered choice. Williams reports in her book that settlers tended to shy away from bear meat if they could help it because the taste was not to their liking.

The nineteenth-century Pacific Northwest was enamored, just like the rest of the United States, with oysters. Understandably so, this region had access to fresh oysters, and locals ate them at home and in restaurants. An 1875 issue of *The Oregonian* features a column-length advertisement for the Oyster Saloon promising fresh Shoalwater Bay Oysters and Eastern Oysters shipped in by steamer and dishes like oyster pan-roasts, raw oysters, and oyster patties.

Over-harvesting caused the local oyster population to dwindle by the late nineteenth century, and locals started using canned oysters instead.

A Dish by Any Other Name

It's obvious that there are regional food differences in the United States. But in some cases those differences may not be as much about a different type of food as a variation of a theme. You may visit a restaurant in a different state that serves dishes you are familiar with, but the restaurant may use unfamiliar names for these dishes.

Consider an American pasta dish that combines macaroni, tomato sauce, and ground beef. In some cases there might be additional ingredients such as onions, garlic, or green bell peppers. What did your mother call this dish? It all depends on where you grew up. People from New England have called it American chop suey. Those from the Midwest call it goulash. Other title variations on this recipe are hunchy gunchy, macaroni casserole, macaroni and beef, and chili mac.

This was a common twentieth-century dish featured in school cafeterias, Army mess halls, and prison cafeterias, and on the dinner table of many people. It's easy to understand why. The ingredients are inexpensive. Variations of the dish can be made so the cook can customize it with any number of vegetables, herbs, or whatever is left in the refrigerator. This recipe for American chop suey, submitted by Mrs. Derby in 1914 for *A Collection of Selected Recipes* by Girl's Friendly Society of Trinity Church, Concord, Massachusetts, shows just one of the ways to cook this dish.

....

AMERICAN CHOP SUEY
  1 lb Hamburg Steak
  1 cup Macaroni
  ½ lb Pork Chop
  1 small can Tomato Soup

Fry an onion in the fat of pork chop, then brown in this the Hamburg steak and pork, which has been cut in pieces. Cover bottom of baking dish with sliced raw potatoes, add a cup of boiled macaroni to the meats, mix thoroughly with tomato soup, cover with bread crumbs and bake. [25]

Notice that this early recipe does not list some of the ingredients (onion, bread crumbs, potatoes) in the list of ingredients. It also lacks information on how to bake the dish or how many people it will feed. These omissions were common in early recipes.

Woodcocks, Snipes, and Peacocks

Today eating local and organic foods is a popular trend. But historically, locally grown food was the only option available to most of the population. Limited food preservation options meant food had to be eaten quickly close to where it was produced or it would spoil. These limitations meant our ancestors couldn't be choosy. They had to eat anything they could find, and they had to make the most of the meat they butchered. The foods they once ate would probably not be as desirable to us. I love to eat my great-grandmother's fudge but not so much my grandmother's head cheese. This section explores unique recipes our ancestors ate to give you an idea of how our tastes have changed over time.

Our ancestors took a different approach to the way they ate. They didn't have the luxury of eating only the parts of the animal that appealed to them. While there are definitely tales of waste in the nineteenth century for example, white hunters would kill buffalo for delicacies like the tongue—our ancestors ate every bit of meat, and that included organs—that are generally undesirable today. During hard economic times, organ meat was a common alternative to more expensive cuts of meat. In addition, organ meat often wasn't rationed like more desirable cuts of meat during wartime. While organs are largely avoided today, it wasn't too long ago that our families ate organ meat and found creative ways to cook it. Consider this recipe from the *Milwaukee Cook Book* by Mrs. J. Magie (1894):

....

BOILED TONGUE WITH TOMATOE SAUCE

Boil a pickled tongue until well done, then skin. For the sauce: One can of tomatoes, boil half down; strain; rub together one tablespoon of butter, one tablespoon of flour, little salt; stir these into the tomato; let it boil; then pour over the tongue and serve.—Mrs. J. B. Oliver[26]

FROG AND TURTLE

Most modern Americans have a limited view of what constitutes meat—beef, pork, fish, and poultry. But our ancestors enjoyed a much wider variety of meats.

Eating frog is not that unusual today, and many fine restaurants sell frog legs. However, the idea of eating frogs in some regions might be reserved for only the most daring diners.

"The only true way to cook a frog is to fry it brown in sweet table butter. First the frog must be dipped in a batter of cracker dust, which should adhere closely when cooked, forming a dainty cracknel of a golden-brown color, with a crisp tang to it when submitted to the teeth. The tender juices retained lose none of their delicate flavor. —Miss Minnie Aikens"[27]

Turtle soup was once a common dish for nineteenth-century Americans but is now more of a regional dish. According to the *Oxford Companion to Food and Drink,* the taste for turtle soup traveled from the Caribbean to England and then to North America. It gained popularity in the latter part of the eighteenth century and early nineteenth century. Prior to the American Civil War, turtles were so plentiful that they were considered slave food in the Southern states. According to the *Oxford Companion,* canned turtle soup was sold in stores by 1882, and by 1911 turtle was one of the higher-priced foods in the United States.[28] It was so popular that there were even recipes for mock turtle soup. In some areas of the United States, you can still hunt and trap turtles during turtle season.

Some nineteenth-century recipes provided information about how to butcher live turtles for the soup, but it must have been a difficult dish to prepare because the turtle's shell makes killing the turtle and harvesting the meat difficult. It was so complicated that the 1848 cookbook *Directions for Cookery, in Its Various Branches* states, "We omit a recipe for *real* turtle soup, as when that very expensive, complicated, and difficult dish is prepared in a private family, it is advisable to hire a first-rate cook for the express purpose."[29] It goes on to suggest that the way to get turtle soup is to buy it from a turtle-soup house.

Turtle meat was expensive, so to cut costs mock turtle soup recipes were created. These recipes used a calf head and feet in place of turtle. It's difficult to understand how a soup made with a calf's head tastes similar to a soup made with turtle meat, but the texture of the meats is said to be similar. Author Christopher Kimball re-created both a traditional and a mock turtle soup in preparation for a re-creation of a Victorian meal. In *Fannie's Last Supper* he says, "Remarkably, the flavor [of the mock soup] reminded me of the turtle soups I had made a few weeks before, but substantially more delicious."[30]

....

TURTLE SOUP

You must have the turtle alive; cut the head off and let it bleed to death. Boil the turtle tilt [*sic*] the shells can be separated, and the meat is cooked. Take off the gall bladder, and if you find a black ball (if there are any) throw it away. Put butter and flour in a sauce pan, and the pieces of turtle and cook a little; pour in some broth; put in your dish a lemon cut in slices, an egg boiled and cut up; pour over it the soup and meat and serve.[31] —from *My Mother's Cook Book*, from the Ladies of St. Louis, compiled for the Women's Christian Home, 1880

....

MOCK TURTLE SOUP

Take the head and two feet, of a calf, that have been carefully cleaned. Separate the jaws and remove the brains. Place the meat in cold water, let it heat slowly, and skim with care. When it is done, take it up, and set it away until the next day. Then skim off the fat, pick the meat from the bones and chop fine; put the liquor and part of the meat in the pot. Tie, in a thin muslin cloth, a few grains of allspice, bruised slightly, and a dozen cloves; add to the soup, also, a grated nutmeg; this is spice enough for a half a gallon of soup. Salt and pepper to taste. Stir frequently to prevent the meat from burning. Half an hour before the soup is done, one tablespoonful of batter, made with water and browned flour, should be added for each gallon; force-meat balls may also be added, if desired. Fifteen minutes before sending to the table, add have [*sic*] a gill of good catsup to each quart of soup. To each gallon, add two tablespoonfulls of lemon juice. The yolks of eight hard-boiled eggs, sliced, should be put in the soup after it is poured into the tureen. This soup may be made equally good with a shank of veal or beef. A little butter and cooked Irish potatoes added to the remaining meat and laid in pie-crust, make a good mock turtle pie.[32] —from *"76": A Cook Book*, edited by the Ladies of Plymouth Church, Des Moines, Iowa, 1876

"Beer is a good family drink." —Lydia Marie Francis Child, 1830

SQUIRREL

While squirrel is something that most Americans would not eat today, it provided an easy meat source for many early Americans. Explorers Lewis and Clark ate squirrel as they traveled the western wilderness. In the November 1, 1921, issue of the *Palm Beach Post* newspaper, the "Timely Recipes" column by Sister Mary included three squirrel recipes. Sister Mary let her readers know that "squirrel pie was an old-fashioned delicacy much relished by our grandfathers." She stated, "Squirrels are delicious cooked with vegetables in a stew" and provided a recipe for squirrel stew.

This squirrel recipe is from the 1885 cookbook *Pittsburgh Tested Recipes*:

....

ROAST RABBIT OR SQUIRREL

Split through the breast and soak one hour in salt water; then put in a pan and slice an onion all over it; sprinkle with celery seed and a little sage and a tablespoonful of butter; place in the oven to roast—Mrs. S. P. Tanner, Frankfort, Ky.[33]

OYSTERS

A few years ago my family was camping in southern California near the coast. To entertain my eight-year-old, I had given him a children's book about the weird foods people eat. He enjoyed looking at the pictures and reading about all kinds of unusual foods people eat in the United States and around the world. One of those foods mentioned was raw oysters. Always the adventurous eater, he asked if he could try some raw oysters because we were so close to their source. Reluctantly, my husband and I, who had never eaten raw oysters, said yes. Though we dreaded it, we ordered raw oysters in a nearby seafood restaurant. The oysters were large and difficult for my eight-year-old to eat; even so, he wanted to try them again the next night. He actually enjoyed the smaller versions and continues to ask for them at seafood restaurants. Because of the texture of oysters and the fact that you have to slurp them rather than chew them, I was shocked that a child would like them.

While today raw oysters are considered a delicacy that often commands a higher price, at one time in America oysters were considered everyday food.

"The two most common gastronomic observations made about nineteenth-century New York were that the oysters were cheap and that the people ate enormous quantities not only [of] oysters but everything."[34]

New Yorkers, as well as others in the United States, ate oysters raw, "stewed, stuffed, fried, roasted, put in soups, or in some way cooked."[35] Recipes for oysters and ways to eat them were endless, including recipes for pickling them. Oysters fell out of fashion and started to become a delicacy in the early 1900s as oyster beds became contaminated. On January 27, 1920, *The New York Times* reported the findings of a state commissioners' report and warned, "Oysters, once plentiful and considered a frugal repast, are gradually being classed as luxuries and will soon become a delicacy."[36]

JELL-O SALADS

Most everyone has had an occasion to enjoy a dessert made of Jell-O. Many people associate Jell-O with salads from the mid-twentieth century, but in reality the method for making a Jell-O type gelatin has been around since 1845 when a patent was taken out for a gelatin dessert preparation created by Peter Cooper. Gelatin was not unknown prior to this time period, but it was a laborious process to create gelatin molds in the nineteenth century. Gelatin was sold in sheets and had to be boiled and prepared with egg whites and shells. The name Jell-O was first coined in 1897 and was sold in fruit flavors.

Today those sweet, fruit-flavored Jell-Os are what most people are familiar with. However, Jell-O, as any company, experimented with a variety of flavors over time and produced recipes for those flavors that might seem strange to modern tastes.

Congealed salads, popular in the mid-twentieth century, served as entrées and relishes and included everything from cheese to meat and fish as well as vegetables. Some ingredients included onions, cabbage, lettuce, radishes, olives, pimentos, bell peppers, celery, tuna, shrimp, and salmon. These salads were often molded.

The following recipe calls for the preparation of the Jell-O and then adding the vinegar, salt, and cayenne and whipping the ingredients together until frothy. Then combine the cheese and mayo and pour into a Jell-O mold and chill. After the Jell-O sets, unmold the salad and garnish with lettuce and more mayo.[37]

....

JELLO-O CHEESE LOAF
  1 package Lemon Jell-O
  1½ cups boiling water
  1 tablespoon vinegar
  1 teaspoon salt

Dash of Cayenne

1 cup grated American cheese or 1 cup cottage cheese or 6 ounces snappy cheese

½ cup mayonnaise

— from *Quick Easy Jell-O Wonder Dishes.* 1930

While some of our ancestors' foods may seem foreign to us, they reflect the tastes of a different era. Knowing the foods that your ancestors enjoyed eating or had to eat when times were tough or food was limited will help you better understand the everyday life of your ancestors.

Notes

» [1] Mark Kurlansky, ed., *The Food of a Younger Land* (New York: Riverhead Books, 2009), 3.

» [2] Ken Albala, *Beans: A History* (New York: Berg, 2007), 165.

» [3] Edward A. Weston, *History of Brooklyn, Susquehanna Co., Penn'a: Its Homes and Its People* (Brooklyn, Pa.: W.A. Squier, 1889), 232.

» [4] John C. Thompson, *History of the Eleventh Regiment, Rhode Island Volunteers, in the war of the rebellion* (Providence, RI: Providence Press Company, 1881), 61.

» [5] Mary Anne DuSablon, *America's Collectible Cookbooks: The History, the Politics, the Recipes* (Athens: Ohio University Press, 1994), 6.

» [6] Janet Clarkson, *Menus from History: Historic Meals and Recipes for Every Day of the Year*, vol. 2 (Santa Barbara, Calif.: Greenwood, 2009), 734.

» [7] Ibid., 740.

» [8] "NYC Statistics," NYC & Company, Inc., http://www.nycgo.com/articles/nyc-statistics-page (accessed October 17, 2011).

» [9] Andrew F. Smith, ed., *The Oxford Companion to American Food and Drink* (Oxford: Oxford University Press, 2007), 414.

» [10] Ibid., 414.

» [11] Ibid., 384.

» [12] Lucy M. Long, *Regional American Food Culture* (Santa Barbara, Calif: Greenwood Press, 2009), 30.

» [13] Ibid., 30.

» [14] Ibid., 31.

» [15] Andrew F. Smith, ed., *The Oxford Companion to American Food and Drink* (Oxford: Oxford University Press, 2007), 554.

» [16] Anne Bower, ed., *African American Foodways: Explorations of History and Culture* (Urbana: University of Illinois Press, 2007), 47.

» [17] Ibid., 48.

» [18] James C. McCann, *Stirring the Pot: A History of African Cuisine* (Athens, Ohio: Ohio University Press, 2009), 167.

» [19] Abby Fisher, *What Mrs. Fisher Knows About Old Southern Cooking, Soups, Pickles, Preserves, Etc.* (San Francisco: Women's Cooperative Printing Office, 1881), 58.

» [20] Lucy M. Long, *Regional American Food Culture* (Santa Barbara, Calif: Greenwood Press, 2009), 37.

» [21] Andrew F. Smith, ed., *The Oxford Companion to American Food and Drink* (Oxford: Oxford University Press, 2007), 556.

» [22] Ibid., 556.

» [23] Ibid., 557.

» [24] Jacqueline B. Williams, *The Way We Ate: Pacific Northwest Cooking, 1843-1900* (Pullman, Washington: Washington State University Press, 1996), xvii.

» [25] Girl's Friendly Society of Trinity Church, Concord, Mass., *A Collection of Selected Recipes* (1914), 9.

» [26] Mrs. J. Magie, *Milwaukee Cook Book* (Milwaukee: Riverside Printing Co., 1894), XX.

» [27] Ibid., 119.

» [28] Andrew F. Smith, ed., *The Oxford Companion to American Food and Drink* (Oxford: Oxford University Press, 2007), 551.

» [29] Eliza Leslie, *Directions for Cookery, in Its Various Branches* (Philadelphia: Carey & Hart, 1848), 31.

» [30] Christopher Kimball, *Fannie's Last Supper: Re-creating One Amazing Meal From Fannie Farmer's 1896 Cookbook* (New York: Hyperion, 2010), 49.

» [31] Women's Christian Home (Saint Louis, Mo.), *My Mother's Cook Book* (Saint Louis: Hugh R. Hildreth Printing Company, 1880), 19.

» [32] The Ladies of Plymouth Church (Des Moines, Iowa), eds., *"76": A Cook Book* (Des Moines, Iowa: Mills, 1876), 14.

» [33] Ladies of Trinity M.E. Church, eds., *Pittsburgh Tested Recipes* (PittsPress of Stevenson & Foster, 1885), 152.

» [34] Mark Kurlansky, ed., *The Food of a Younger Land*, Large-print edition (New York: Riverhead Books, 2009), 369.

» [35] Ibid., 382.

» [36] Ibid., 446.

» [37] Jell-O Co., Inc., *Quick, Easy Jell-O Wonder Dishes* (New York: General Foods Corp., 1930), 14.

*From
the
Family
Kitchen*

51

PART 1
CH. 3

CHAPTER 4

Food Throughout Time

"We suffered greatly for the want of salt; but,
by burning the outside of our mule steaks,
and sprinkling a little gunpowder upon them,
it did not require a very extensive stretch of
the imagination to fancy the presence of
both salt and pepper." —RANDOLPH BARNES MARCY, 1859

Today it's trendy to eat locally grown and locally produced foods, but our ancestors had little choice but to eat what they could grow and produce in their communities. It's only thanks to modern transportation methods and food preservation techniques that we are able to enjoy fresh ingredients from all over the world. This chapter explores how diets have been affected by technology, location, and social and political events such as depression and war.

Technology Changed How We Eat

American diets have evolved greatly since the country was founded, thanks to a number of advances in technology. While this book cannot go into an entire food history, we'll look at a few key inventions that significantly changed the way we eat.

CAST IRON STOVES

Developed in the eighteenth century, cast iron stoves completely changed the way food was cooked and prepared. By the end of the Civil War, most American homes had a cast iron stove.[1] This was a significant upgrade from cooking over an open fire. Cooking could be done both inside the stove and on the cooking range on top of the stove. It allowed women to cook more elaborate meals with more than one hot course. While these were clearly advantages over previous cooking methods—a pot suspended in the fireplace—these stoves were wood-burning, so regulating the temperature was a challenge.

REFRIGERATION

Prior to iceboxes, the gathering and preserving of food was a full-time job. Starting in the early 1800s, the advent of iceboxes for the home helped women keep food fresher longer and reduced the need for preservation methods like salting or drying. This was a huge time-saver because food could be collected in bulk and kept fresh without labor-intensive preservation methods.

Susan Strasser, the author of *Never Done: A History of American Housework*, describes the process of sending the ice to customers for their iceboxes. It was harvested in huge blocks from frozen lakes in the north and then stored in icehouses until it was shipped for either local delivery (available in cities from ice carts making regular rounds by the 1850s) or long-distance transport.[2] While the wealthy started purchasing iceboxes in the early 1800s, iceboxes were still fairly rare for most families until the latter part of the 1800s. Iceboxes gave way to the refrigerator in the early 1900s. Some of the first refrigerators were as expensive as a new car. By the end of World War II, iceboxes were a thing of the past.[3]

RAILROAD

The transcontinental railroad was completed in 1869 and linked the entire United States. Prior to that, railroads were local and regional ventures with limited range because of ownership and gauge discrepancies. Invented in the late 1850s and patented in the 1860s, refrigerator cars, also known as reefers, used ice to transport perishables. These cars allowed meat to be transported safely, doing away with driving cattle from places like Texas to the East. With refrigerated cars, food perishables like meat, dairy, fruit, and beer could be transported and sold anywhere in the country. Regional foods could now spread easily across the country. A lobster caught on the East Coast could be shipped to the Midwest and enjoyed by diners there.

AGRICULTURE

Innovations in agricultural technology made it easier to plant, harvest, and send produce to market. Innovations such as crop rotation helped preserve the fertility of the land and maximize crop yield. George Washington Carver used crop rotation to help the South after decades of overplanting tobacco and cotton. Mechanical innovations, such as the tractor, grain elevator, hay baler, and combine, allowed more land to be cleared, planted, and harvested in time and with a smaller workforce.

CANNED FOOD

Not everyone would see canned food as an important contribution to our ancestors' lives. But what we take for granted today gave our ancestors easy access to a variety of foods, regardless of growing season or location. Canning allows food to be stored for longer periods of time, up to five years for most foods, a vast improvement over other preserving methods. Canning was first developed in 1810 to help Napoleon feed his troops. Considering that canning was developed during a war, it's no surprise that it was heavily relied on during times of war in the United States when food shortages were looming. During World War II, canned goods were rationed. Consider this news story in the February 20, 1943, issue of the Eugene, Oregon, *Register-Guard*: "Don't hoard, but buy today all the canned fruits and vegetables you'll need next week because none may be sold legally from midnight tonight until the morning of March 1." It adds, "Canned meat and canned fish, whose sale was stopped Wednesday night, will be rationed along with fresh meat."

PRESERVATION

While canning is one way to preserve foods, historically people have used other ways to keep food fresher longer out of necessity. Other methods include drying, salting, pickling, smoking, and chemicals.

DRYING

Beef jerky is probably one of most familiar dried foods. Modern technology has made drying a less popular form of food preservation, but this ancient food preservation method was important to our ancestors.

Drying works by removing all the water in a food item, and that moisture removal prevents spoiling. Drying food can be accomplished by hanging food in direct sunlight, heating it, or exposing it to dry air.

SALTING

Today, we are advised to avoid salt, but that wasn't the case for our ancestors. Salt was used for everything from tanning leather and keeping work animals healthy to preserving food. In fact, using salt to preserve food is pretty much universal practice throughout the world.[4] Salt preserves food in two ways: It draws water out of the food, and it destroys bacterial and fungal cells. "Salt controls fermentation, wherein the safe, 'good' bacteria already existing in the food breaks apart sugars to create an acid. The acid helps preserve the food for extended periods . . ."[5].

A passage in the John Steinbeck novel *The Grapes of Wrath* describes the process of salting meat: "Noah carried the slabs of meat into the kitchen and cut it into small salting blocks, and Ma patted the coarse salt in, laid it piece by piece in the kegs, careful that no two pieces touched each other. She laid the slabs like bricks, and pounded salt in the spaces."

Today we still eat food preserved in salt, including corned beef, pastrami, ham, cod, and dried beef.

PICKLING

The word *pickle* instantly conjures up the image of cucumbers stuffed in a jar. Pickling also brings to mind other products that are sold pickled, like eggs, hot peppers, okra, green beans, onions, hot dogs, and even pigs' feet. Pickling is a historical preservation method that involves soaking food in vinegar to kill and keep out bacteria.[6]

Pickling has been popular in all parts of the world including Asian and Middle Eastern countries. Pickling became popular in sixteenth-century England when salted food was losing favor with the upper classes; salted food soon became associated with the poor.

Pickling all kinds of vegetables allowed harvests to last longer in a household. Most early cookbooks had a pickle and relish section that included much more than just cucumber pickles. An 1876 cookbook includes pickling recipes for fruits and vegetables—green tomatoes, onions, green peppers, cabbage, cauliflower, cherries, currants, grapes, apples, plums, and peaches.[7] During World Wars I and II, Americans pickled food they grew in their victory gardens to help make food available year-round instead of only in season.[8]

SMOKING

Smoking meats, poultry, and fish originated in prehistoric times.[9] It employs the same principle as drying, removing moisture to reduce spoilage. Meats that were not drying in a timely manner were hung by a fire. Food was also hung over the chimney to be smoked. Smoke has many chemicals, including formaldehyde, that act as inhibitors to the growth of microbes.[10]

CHEMICALS

Today we are concerned about chemicals in our foods, and most grocery stores and markets carry a selection of organic foods free of pesticides and chemicals. But, chemicals have been used to preserve and cure food—lutefisk, for example—since long before the advent of modern convenience food.

56

Lutefisk is cod preserved in lye, a corrosive alkaline substance that in the past was made from hardwood ashes. The lye used in curing foods such as green olives is a food-grade lye. How this method of curing fish originated is surrounded in legend, but the fish is now eaten by those with Swedish and Norwegian ancestry. In the United States, lutefisk is served at church dinners in states like Wisconsin and Minnesota. Lutefisk takes fifteen days to prepare: Dried codfish is soaked in water for a week, with the water being changed each day. Then the lye solution is added, and the fish soaks in that for four days. The lye solution is poured off, and the fish is soaked in water for four more days, the water being changed each morning. Once ready, the fish is boiled before serving.[11]

WESTWARD EXPANSION

As Americans answered the call of manifest destiny and pushed toward the West, their diets shifted from local and homegrown food to shelf-stable food that could sustain them as they traveled for months across the Oregon or Mormon trails. While some provisions could be acquired along the way at trading posts or by hunting, most of the food had to be packed, and they had to make sure their supplies would not run out. Lots of advice was given to those wanting to make the trek west. In 1845, author Lansford

W. Hastings wrote *The Emigrants' Guide to Oregon and California*. In it he recommended that the emigrants take "two hundred pounds of flour, or meal; one hundred and fifty pounds of bacon; ten pounds of coffee; twenty pounds of sugar; and ten pounds of salt, with such other provisions as he may prefer, and can conveniently take; the provisions above enumerated, are considered ample, both as to quantity and variety." He also pointed out that pistols were useful when you saw buffalo because you could "gollop [*sic*] your horse, side by side, with them, and having pistols, you may shoot them down at your pleasure."[12]

The *Nauvoo Neighbor* newspaper suggested Mormons traveling in 1845 equip themselves with one thousand pounds of flour or other bread or bread stuffs, one pound tea, five pounds coffee, one hundred pounds sugar, one pound cayenne pepper, two pounds black pepper, half a pound of mustard, ten pounds rice, one pound cinnamon, half a pound of cloves, one dozen nutmegs, twenty-five pounds salt, five pounds saleratus (a precursor to baking soda), ten pounds dried apples, half a bushel of beans, a few pounds of dried beef or bacon, and five pounds dried peaches.[13]

ECONOMIC CRISIS

Mention the Great Depression and most people have images of the Dust Bowl and migrant workers living in shacks. They visualize the famous photograph by Dorothea Lange entitled *Migrant Mother* that shows a worried mother with two small children. For some, the Depression may have been a time when their family moved, looking for a better life, trying to escape extreme poverty. For others, the Depression may have felt no different because poverty was a fact of life. As families struggled to avoid homelessness and provide the necessities for their families, how and what did they eat? In *Clara's Kitchen: Wisdom, Memories, and Recipes From the Great Depression*, Clara Cannucciari explained, "We just relied on what we did have—the ability to sacrifice and put our needs into perspective. To be resourceful about what we got. And by preparing and eating simple, filling foods."[14]

Families of the Depression era relied on inexpensive foods and what could be grown at home or gathered. Foods procured from home or through other gathering methods are always cheaper than those in a store. Vegetables, rather than meat, became a staple. Eggs provided cheap protein for families with chickens. Families may have even gathered foods, from picking wild berries or nuts to picking what we would today call weeds to be eaten as vegetables. My maternal grandmother raised nine children and was used to living with very little. One day she took my dad on a tour in our backyard and explained what weeds could be used as food and how to prepare them. Eating weeds such as dandelion greens, stinging nettle, purslane, and ground ivy has a long history. Recipes featuring these plants appear in early cookbooks. While there is a movement now to incorporate weeds into cooking, I recommend extreme caution if you decide to harvest weeds today because of possible contamination from herbicides and pesticides.

AMERICA EATS

In the 1930s, the Works Progress Administration (WPA)—a part of President Franklin D. Roosevelt's New Deal—paid writers and photographers to chronicle the foodways of average Americans. The goal of the project, titled "America Eats," was to document food served at community events across the United States. It was not a cookbook, but instead the writers interviewed local cooks about ingredients, preparation, and the origins of their dishes. Imagine all the wonderful information this project provided future genealogists.

Unfortunately, due to budget cuts and politics, "America Eats" was never published. The writers were told to send all materials to the Library of Congress (LOC) for archiving, and many did, but many writers sent their material to state repositories, where they are still archived or were destroyed.

Search the Library of Congress card catalog at <catalog.loc.gov> for materials from the "America Eats" program. You can also find photographs from the "America Eats" project through the Library of Congress Prints and Photographs Online Catalog at <www.loc.gov/pictures/item/00649983>.

In some cases, manuscripts or copies of manuscripts were sent to other repositories. One example comes from the Montana State University Library's collection of WPA records that includes manuscripts from the "America Eats" program <www.lib.montana.edu/collect/spcoll/findaid/2336.html>. These records contain documents created from the Montana division of the WPA as well as Nevada, Oregon, Idaho, Colorado, South Dakota, and Wyoming. The "America Eats" pages in this collection include recipes, correspondence, and research materials.

You can look through manuscript collections at state archives and libraries as well as university libraries. There are several ways to research a manuscript collection. One is to search through each repository's individual catalog. Another is to search several catalogs through the National

Union Catalog of Manuscript Collections (NUCMC) <www.loc.gov/coll/nucmc/index.html>. Click on the link List of Participating Repositories to see which libraries, museums, and archives participate in NUCMC. When searching a catalog for materials related to the "America Eats" project, try using keywords like *WPA*, *Works Progress Administration*, or *America Eats*.

In recent years, some of the pages from "America Eats" have been published as part of books on the history of the project. Three such books are *America Eats* by Pat Willard, *The Food of a Younger Land* edited by Mark Kurlansky, and *America Eats* by Nelson Algren.

"America Eats" was an important project spotlighting regional food differences in a different era. Today there are many ways to learn about regional food differences, whether on the internet or through a cookbook. During the time of the "America Eats" project and for years after, writers like Sheila Hibben wrote about regional foods. Writer Clementine Paddleford even learned how to pilot a plane just so she could taste and write about food found throughout the United States.

WAR

War has greatly impacted diets throughout history. Blockades, occupied zones, disrupted transportation lines, and destruction of cropland and farm animals quickly create food shortages. If your ancestors lived through a war, that war likely affected how and what they ate.

CIVIL WAR SHORTAGES

Food shortages were a crippling reality in the South during the Civil War. Even in the beginning of the war, there was a risk of soldiers deserting due to lack of food. As the war progressed, it became worse. As the war continued, the South was literally starved into defeat. Shortages caused food prices to become so outrageous that all but the wealthy were starving. Even the soldiers were not given their rations. Confederate soldiers wrote home of having no rations or enduring half rations after battles. Starving soldiers were forced to eat mules and rats. One Confederate major wrote that a market in Vicksburg was selling both mule and rat meat and that rats were priced at $2.50 (roughly $44 today). At different times there were also reports of civilians and soldiers eating dogs and cats.[15]

Women were writing to their soldier husbands about the lack of food available to their families. In a letter from Confederate Captain John Bell (Company H, 32nd Alabama Infantry) to his wife Nancy (Robinson), he refers to some of the reports of starvation he has heard:

I am glad too, to hear that the crop looks so well. If we can only make enough to live on during the war, and enjoy good health I shall be satisfied. It would grieve me very much however, to receive such letters from you, as I saw some women write to their husbands, stating that they have neither meat nor bread and no means of procuring any. Some women have actually left their homes and came to the camps bringing their children with them, and are now engaged as laundresses. Each company is allowed to draw rations for four women when engaged as laundresses.
—Capt. John Bell, June 15, 1862[16]

One of the most crippling shortages the South faced almost from the beginning of the war was salt. The versatility of salt made it a priceless substance. It was used to preserve meats, fish, and butter and to tan leather goods. Farmers needed it to provide electrolytes to their horses and cows. According to *Starving the South*, Southerners used 450 million pounds of salt each year at the outbreak of the Civil War.[17] While there was limited salt production in the United States at this time (more in the North than in the South), most was shipped in from Europe. Days after the start of the Civil War, President Abraham Lincoln ordered a blockade of all Southern ports, thus cutting off supplies of many goods, including salt.

60

Cavalry horses became ill, cows didn't fatten up, and pork could not be processed.[18] The South tried numerous ways to capture residue salt, including evaporating seawater, reusing crystals that fell off of salted meats, boiling down brine that had been used in pickling, and boiling planks of wood used in salt houses.[19] Between the lack of salt and the speculators driving up prices for what little salt was available, salt became so precious that small packets of it were given as gifts.

As the food shortages continued, bread riots began breaking out in Confederate cities, and women were the main participants. Tales of the bread riots expanded and were sometimes embellished by Northern papers, perhaps to show how much better things were for the North and to prove how the South couldn't win the war. Sometimes the retelling of these riots down played the real concern of starving women and children in the South. In its coverage of the bread riots in Richmond, Virginia, *The New York Times* reported that the woman in charge of the rioting was a "tall, daring, Amazonian-looking woman, who had a white feather standing erect from her hat, and who was evidently directing the movements of the plunderers."[20] Bread riots occurred because, despite the pay their soldier husbands were due and the money they earned through their own work, women couldn't afford food. Blockades and speculators caused food prices to rise dramatically. For example, bacon typically cost $1.25 a pound, but in February 1863 bacon cost $10 a pound.[21] Women in various cities started rioting and yelling chants like "Bread or Blood."

WORLD WARS I AND II

The Civil War is but one example of how food plays an integral part in war. While more of an extreme example, other wars have also affected access to food. While World War I did cause some changes in the way Americans ate (for example, food rationing was experimented with), World War II had a more recent and lasting impact on the way Americans eat. To conserve supplies for those fighting the war, civilians were encouraged to do their share by growing their own foods in victory gardens, taking part in rationing, and skipping meat on Meatless Tuesdays.

CHANGING ROLE OF WOMEN

Women played a large role in the war effort, even during the earlier years when their political voice was silenced by their disenfranchisement. One way British women assisted the effort was through the work of the Women's Land Army.

The "farmerette" took over the farm work for men who were called to serve in the military during World War I. The farmerettes did everything from planting, plowing, and harvesting fields to hauling lumber. Fears of food shortages and high prices led these women to organize themselves and take over the work of men. While women had always worked on farms, this was the first time they were paid for their work. Women were organized in camps and participated in training, including physical training prior to working. Most men did not accept that women could do hard farm work at first, but over time and with equalizers like tractors, these women showed they were capable, and they helped Britain fend off an agriculture crisis. During World War II, the Women's Land Army was resurrected in Britain, as well as the United States and Australia, to take over farms once again as the men marched off to war.

Women also filled factory jobs left vacant by men serving in the military. These "Rosie the Riveters" worked long hours outside the home, which left little time for them to prepare meals. By the time their husbands came home from the war, women were used to cooking with the time-saving conveniences of canned foods, frozen meals, and mixes.

RATIONING

On the home front, Americans made countless sacrifices to support the war effort. Rationing was common and affected all types of consumer goods, including gas, tires, and nylon stockings. But the most difficult rationing to deal with was food.

Imagine being told by the government the quantity and type of food you could buy. While food rationing was voluntary during World War I, it was mandatory for U.S. civilians during World War II. Several types of food staples were rationed, including sugar, meat, cheese, butter, coffee, and canned foods.

The United Kingdom also had food rationing during the war and, because of low food supplies, continued the practice until 1954. While rationing in the United States ended at the end of the war, after the war President Harry S. Truman introduced food conservation as a way Americans could help those in European countries who were going hungry.

Marketing campaigns used posters, magazines, and newsreels to sell rationing as a patriotic duty. Women were encouraged to do all they could to keep the soldiers fed, including rationing, growing their own food, reducing food waste, and preserving harvests.

COOKBOOKS ON RATIONING

Cookbooks produced during World War II show the effects of rationing. A recipe booklet published by the Metropolitan Life Insurance Company reflects the sentiment of the war effort: "The scarcest foods are rationed so that all of us will have a fair share." The book suggests making the most of meals by "using the same foods in a variety of ways, using leftovers, and cooking foods so that all of their original value will be preserved."[22]

Many cookbooks of this era were produced specifically to help women make the most of the limited variety and quantity of foods they had. They also offered substitutions for foods no longer available due to rationing. Recipe titles often used the word *mock* to indicate substitutions made in the dish. Meat was the most common ingredient that was substituted.

These cookbooks also provided ideas and techniques for preparing less expensive and less desirable cuts of meat. For example, recipes substituting beef suggested different meats, including those that most people were unaccustomed to eating. One wartime recipe flyer encouraged readers to eat pork hearts, feet, brains, knuckles, kidneys, liver, and backbone in place of more traditional cuts of pork. Less desirable cuts of meat not only saved consumers money but also cost fewer ration coupons.

The Metropolitan Life Insurance Company cookbook has this sugges-
tion for making the most of limited quantities of meat: "meat extenders,
like cereal, bread crumbs, soybeans and soybean grits, and vegetables,
help to use leftovers and make low-cost cuts attractive."[23] Housewives were
reminded that "brains, sweetbreads, tripe, liver, heart, tongue, and oxtail
are known as variety meats. They are high in food value …"

One example of a recipe created to help a housewife make the most of
her leftovers is the following:

....

MINCED MEAT ON TOAST

Use any meat, put through a food grinder or chop fine in a chopping
bowl. Heat in gravy, white sauce, or tomato sauce. Add butter, season well,
and serve on hot toast.[24]

VICTORY GARDENS

As a response to food rationing, civilians began to grow and preserve their
own vegetables and fruits. Known as victory gardens, these home gardens
were cultivated during both World War I and World War II. Gardens were
planted in public and private places and were of varying sizes, everything
from small planters to parks or rooftops. They gave families ready access to
produce along with the option to can and preserve that produce for future
use. It was one way to make up for shortages and preserve ration coupons
for hard-to-come-by items. Both the government and private industry
launched marketing campaigns to encourage victory gardens. During
World War II there were as many as twenty million gardens in the United
States.

The Role of Betty Crocker

The 1950s marked a time of many innovations in the kitchen. Women had
worked outside the home during the war years, but when the war ended
and the men returned, women were sent back home to be the "ultimate"
housekeepers. Cooks in the 1950s demanded two things from foods—
convenience and presentation.

Women cooking in the 1950s had a lot of help—not help as in a maid,
but help as in convenience foods. Betty Crocker, a 1920s brand persona
for the Washington Grosby Company (the precursor to General Mills),
answered women's cooking questions. Betty Crocker was popular and often
thought to be a real woman (although several women did act as Betty Crocker
for promotional activities like answering letters and radio and television

*From
the
Family
Kitchen*

63

PART 1
CH. 4

appearances). She was so popular that in 1945 she was voted the second-best-known woman, after Eleanor Roosevelt, by *Fortune* magazine.[25]

Many families may have tasted dishes cooked from the Betty Crocker *Picture Cook Book*. First published in 1950, this cookbook quickly became a bestseller and included iconic dishes such as Chili Con Carne, Spaghetti, Snickerdoodles, Eggs Benedict, Pot Roast, and Apple Pie.

Food Now and in the Future

Our more recent food history spans decades of television cooking shows, the increased availability of ethnic cuisines, the increasing access to prepared and convenience foods, the frequency of eating out, and the availability of a variety of organic and exotic ingredients. While earlier generations relied solely on either cookbooks or recipes from friends and family, today the internet makes it easier than ever to find a recipe and ingredients from any part of the world.

An important part of gathering and preserving family history is preserving our family traditions now. The foods we eat today and the celebrations that mean so much to our families can and will change over time. Foods your children eat today may be forgotten by their families twenty years from now. People die before we can ask them questions. Memories fade and we simply can't find answers. We take everyday life for granted. Because it is so familiar, we fail to record it. Writing down your favorite family recipes and food traditions will help keep that information fresh for future generations. Make a commitment to take some time to preserve these present-day memories so they will be available for the future. Document the foods you eat at holiday celebrations. Include recipes for family favorites. Take photos of your kitchen, cooking tools, and favorite foods.

Notes

» [1] Laura Schenone, *The Lost Ravioli Recipes of Hoboken: A Search for Food and Family* (New York: Norton & Co., 2008), 183.

» [2] Susan Strasser, *Never Done: A History of American Housework* (New York: Pantheon Books, 1982), 19.

» [3] Andrew F. Smith, ed., *The Oxford Companion to American Food and Drink* (Oxford: Oxford University Press, 2007), 313.

» [4] Sue Shephard, *Pickled, Potted, and Canned: How the Art and Science of Food Preserving Changed the World* (New York: Simon & Schuster, 2000), 75.

» [5] Andrew F. Smith, ed., *The Oxford Companion to American Food and Drink* (Oxford: Oxford University Press, 2007), 518.

» [6] Sue Shephard, *Pickled, Potted, and Canned: How the Art and Science of Food Preserving Changed the World* (New York: Simon & Schuster, 2000), 95.

» [7] The Ladies of Plymouth Church (Des Moines, Iowa), eds., *"76": A Cook Book* (Des Moines, Iowa: Mills, 1876), 225.

» [8] Andrew F. Smith, ed., *The Oxford Companion to American Food and Drink* (Oxford: Oxford University Press, 2007), 453.

» [9] Ibid., 543.

» [10] Sue Shephard, *Pickled, Potted, and Canned: How the Art and Science of Food Preserving Changed the World* (New York: Simon & Schuster, 2000), 109.

» [11] Mark Kurlansky, ed., *The Food of a Younger Land,* Large-print edition (New York: Riverhead Books, 2009), 265.

» [12] Langsford W. Hastings, *The Emigrants' Guide to Oregon and California* (Cincinnati: George Conclin, 1845), 143.

» [13] William W. Slaughter and Michael Landon, *Trail of Hope: The Story of the Mormon Trail* (Salt Lake City: Deseret Book Co., 1997), 23.

» [14] Clara Cannucciari, *Clara's Kitchen: Wisdom, Memories, and Recipes From the Great Depression* (New York: St. Martin's Press, 2009), 1.

» [15] Andrew F. Smith, ed., *Starving the South: How the North Won the Civil War* (New York: St. Martin's Press, 2011), 164.

» [16] John W. Bell Papers, MSS 771, 1862–1864. Louisiana Lower Mississippi Valley Collections, Hill Memorial Library, Louisiana State University.

» [17] Andrew F. Smith, ed., *Starving the South: How the North Won the Civil War* (New York: St. Martin's Press, 2011), 32.

» [18] Ibid., 38.

» [19] Mark Kurlansky, ed., *The Food of a Younger Land* (New York: Riverhead Books, 2009), 269.

» [20] "Richmond's Bread Riot Jefferson Davis Describes a War-Time Incident," *The New York Times,* 30 April 1889.

» [21] Andrew F. Smith, ed., *Starving the South: How the North Won the Civil War* (New York: St. Martin's Press, 2011), 83.

» [22] Metropolitan Life Insurance Co., *Metropolitan Cook Book,* (New York: Metropolitan Life Insurance Co., 1942), 2.

» [23] Ibid., 2.

» [24] Ibid., 29.

» [25] Susan Marks, *Finding Betty Crocker: The Secret Life of America's First Lady of Food* (New York: Simon & Schuster, 2005), 115.

CHAPTER 5

Cookbooks and Menus

"In fact, women formally constructed their matrilineal genealogies and their relationships to one another in their cookbooks, binding together the different generations."
—JANET THEOPHANO, 2002

Have you ever thought about the cookbooks on your shelf? They may have been given to you as gifts. Perhaps they were passed down from family members, or maybe you purchased them yourself. The cookbook has evolved from its beginnings as a domestic handbook to glossy, heavily photographed books with creative recipes that transport the reader to a different locale.

Cookbooks are one of the most popular genres of books sold.[1] Enter any bookstore and you will find dozens of shelves and complete sections devoted to cookbooks written by numerous types of authors—celebrity chefs with their own television empires, restaurant chefs sharing recipes, compilation books filled with recipes from contributors, and cookbooks from grocery stores. Given the star power of many of the authors, it's not surprising that modern cookbooks are often purchased as entertainment items instead of reference material. Many cookbook enthusiasts read a cookbook cover to cover rather than just use it as a reference work. Today you can find cookbooks for ethnic groups, religious groups, dieters, vegetarians and vegans, devotees of unusual foods and ingredients (like the cookbook I bought at an aquarium on cooking with seaweed), and those devoted to only one type of food such as cheeses or sandwiches. It's easy to take their format, their colorful pictures, and their tempting recipes for granted.

As you look through your own family's collection of cookbooks, you will notice that they provide information about how to prepare and cook certain ingredients along with ideas for meal planning and entertaining. While vintage mass-market cookbooks provide some ideas of what foods were available and what people ate when the book was published, they may not be accurate representations of what people actually did eat. Just as you probably have cookbooks on your shelf that contain recipes you would never actually cook, the same would have been true of our ancestors. Cookbooks often taught an ideal that was not always practiced by the women who owned them. When looking at old cookbooks for clues to what your ancestor ate, remember that some recipes show the author's creativity rather than what real people actually ate. But they're still good ways to get an idea of food trends and available foods of a time period.

A History of Cookbooks

Americans have always had access to cookbooks, though the first one written by an American wasn't published until 1796. Prior to that Americans had two choices for acquiring cookbooks. They could purchase cookbooks from England, including *The Compleat Housewife; or Accomplished Gentlewoman's Companion* by Eliza Smith (1730), *The Art of Cookery, Made Plain and Easy* by Hannah Glasse (1747), and *The Frugal Housekeeper: or, Complete Woman Cook* by Susannah Carter (1772). While these would have been helpful in the colonies, they would have lacked an important component, namely an explanation of how to cook foods native to this new land.

The second option for colonials was to compile recipes. While colonial cooks could purchase cookbooks from England, they most likely compiled their own collections in notebooks filled with blank pieces of paper. Known as manuscript cookbooks, these books were works in progress where cooks made comments, updates, and added information that may not have been focused solely on cooking. Recipes added to the pages were created by the cook, her family, and her friends. These manuscript cookbooks "became a record of the individuals to whom they were connected through kinship and through other alliances."[2]

As you study cooking through the ages, you will find manuscript cookbooks being used by women in the early twentieth century as they attend cooking classes and document their own recipes as well as those from their social circle. This tradition continued throughout the twentieth century as women documented recipes on 3" x 5" recipe cards for personal use and to give to others. Maybe you have a recipe box filled with recipes from relatives, friends, and your own kitchen. In some ways the manuscript book tradition continues with the advent of community cookbooks compiled with recipes from a community of women. In the twenty-first century the manuscript cookbook tradition continues but has gone digital and moved online in the form of blogs. The internet lets cooks from around the world share recipes with each other with just the click of a mouse.

The first cookbook written by an American for an American audience was *American Cookery, or the Art of Dressing Viands, Fish, Poultry, and Vegetables, and the Best Modes of Making Puffs-Pastes, Pies, Tarts, Puddings, Custards, and Preserves, and All Kinds of Cakes, From the Imperial Plumb to Plain Cake, Adapted to This Country, and All Grades of Life* by Amelia Simmons, published in 1796. While not much is known about Simmons, we do know that, like many authors of her time, she borrowed recipes from other cookbooks. But her cookbook was the first to include foods native to America and is thought to be the first to "record recipes for pumpkin pie, Indian pudding, cramberry [*sic*] tart and Indian slapjacks."[3]

In addition to providing recipes, *American Cookery* also explained how to choose meat, produce, and other foodstuffs and, when necessary, how to butcher meat. There are detailed instructions on killing and preparing a turtle, a popular soup ingredient even into the modern day. While most of the foods mentioned in Simmons's book are ones modern Americans would be familiar with like beef, turkey, lamb, oysters, onions, and carrots, other foods would not be standard fare served in today's American kitchens, such as turtle, eel, or peacock.

The format of the book would also be unfamiliar to modern cooks, for example, a recipe for bread pudding:

BREAD PUDDING

One pound soft bread or biscuit soaked in one quart milk, run thro' a sieve or cullender, add 7 eggs, three quarters of a pound sugar, one quarter of a pound butter, nutmeg or cinnamon, one gill rose-water, one pound stoned raisons, half pint cream, bake three quarters of an hour, middling oven.[4]

Today's recipes include a title, introduction, serving size, ingredient list, complete directions (including cooking time, temperature, and exact measurements), and notes. Historical recipes, like this one for bread pudding, read more like a narrative. Some measurements are given, but not for every ingredient. There are also no instructions on how to cut or mix the ingredients, what to cook them in, and at what temperature to cook them.

Recipe writers in the eighteenth and parts of the nineteenth century assumed their readers would have some skills that would inform the way they followed the recipe. Christopher Kimball illustrates this point in his 2010 book *Fannie's Last Supper*. He describes his process of cooking a calf's head for mock turtle soup. The first batch he made tasted horrible, and he realized that the Victorian-era recipe he was following didn't include some of the details needed to properly prepare and cook the head—specifically removing the brains, a step that a cook in the Victorian era would just know.[5]

COOK, CLEAN, AND COMFORT

Since their beginnings, cookbooks have been a resource to consult for recipes. But early cookbooks also served as household manuals full of housekeeping tips and medicinal remedies, information that a homemaker would need. According to author Mary Barile, "Cookery books, imported or homemade, represented more than recipes to colonial women; they were important links with home [and] sometimes the only sources available for domestic and medicinal information."[6]

Cookbooks included recipes for folk remedies, antidotes to ingested poisons, and advice for taking care of children, the sick, and injured. This information was typically found in the back of the book, after all of the food recipes. This information became very important to women in the late nineteenth century when many households moved west to areas far from their support system including family, friends, and doctors.

Products of their era, the titles of some of these medicinal recipes may seem strange to us now. Consider such remedies as For a Felon (ointment for sores), Calendula Salve for Caked Breast (for mothers who are sore from breast-feeding), and Cure for a Wen (wens are boils or cysts).

The recipe for Hot Drops, an all-round cure, uses alcohol as a major part of the curative, similar to many medicinal recipes found in older cookbooks.

....

HOT DROPS

One gallon of best brandy, one pound gum myrrh, quarter pound of powdered cayenne pepper; shake every day for a week or so.

Dose- Half a teaspoonful stirred into a little sugar, pour on to it, one cup boiling water; drink hot. Be sure to mix the liquid with the sugar, before pouring on the water. These drops are good for almost everything, a gallon is none too much to prepare at one time. The best household remedy that there is; it has been used for fifty years in a New England family. – Mrs. Evelyn Whiting, Marblehead, Mass.[7]

Cookbooks also included tips to help with the running of a household including housecleaning and laundry. They included recipes for household cleaners, stain removers, and hand and laundry soap. The following recipe was for cleaning clothes:

....

SOAP BARK FOR CLEANING DRESS GOODS

Get ten cents worth of bark, steep it into one gallon of water, wash the goods in that water same as you would clothes; steep same bark over to rinse in; takes out all grease stains, makes goods look like new; dampen and press. – Mrs. W. H. Eldred, Chicago[8]

A DASH OF PRACTICAL ADVICE

Mock recipes, not to be confused with recipes for ingredient substitutions also labeled as mock recipes, are recipes for living and were used in cookbooks throughout the twentieth century. Their goal was to offer advice on domestic issues in a non-preaching sort of way. You'll find many of the same mock recipes repeated in numerous cookbooks. They teach everything from how to live a better life to how to treat your spouse. One of the most popular has been the recipe for How to Cook a Husband.

How to Cook a Husband

A good many husbands are ruined by mismanagement. Some women go about as if their husbands were bladders, and blow them up. Others keep them constantly in hot water; others let them freeze by their carelessness and influence. Some keep them in a stew by

irritating ways and words. Others roast them. Some keep them in a pickle all their lives.
It cannot be supposed that any husband will be tender and good managed in this way,
but they are really delicious when properly treated. In selecting your husband you should
not be guided by the silvery appearance, as in buying mackerel, nor by the golden tint,
as if you wanted salmon. Be sure and select him yourself, as the tastes differ. Do not
go to the market for him, as the best are always brought to your door. It is far better to
have none unless you patiently learn how to cook him. A preserving kettle of the finest
porcelain is best, but if you have nothing but an earthenware pipkin it will do, with
care. See that the linen in which you wrap him is nicely washed and mended, with the
required number of buttons and strings nicely sewed on. Tie him in the kettle by a strong
silk cord called comfort, as the one called duty is apt to be weak. They are apt to fly out
of the kettle and be burned and crusty on the edges, since, like crabs and lobsters, you
have to cook them alive. Make a clear, steady fire out of love, neatness and cheerful-
ness. Set him as near this as seems to agree with him. If he sputters and fizzes do not be
anxious; some husbands do this til they are quite done. Add a little sugar in the form of
what confectionaries [sic] call kisses, but no vinegar or pepper on any account. A little
spice proves them, but it must be used with judgment. Do not stick any sharp instruments
into him to see if he is becoming tender. Stir him gently; watch the while, lest he lie too
close and flat to the kettle, and so become useless. You cannot fail to know when he is
done. If thus treated you will find him very digestible, agreeing nicely with you and the
children, and he will keep as long as you want, unless you become careless and you set
him in too cold of a place. [9]

From
the
Family
Kitchen

71

PART 1
CH. 5

Cookbooks have really been encyclopedias of wisdom. Whether they provide recipes for cooking and nourishing a family, tips on how to keep your home and laundry clean, how to cure what ails your family, or advice for living, cookbooks have always been more than reference books; they are everyday guides to life.

THE MODERN COOKBOOK

Flip through several different modern cookbooks and you'll see there is a standard formula for how recipes are written. This wasn't always the case. As previously mentioned, when cookbooks were first introduced, recipes were presented in whatever format the author or publisher chose. They also lacked standard measurements, meaning a pinch in one cookbook did not always equal a pinch in another cookbook.

Cooking took a turn at the height of the Industrial Revolution. It was a time when scientific discoveries and advances were greatly influencing daily life in everything from work to housekeeping. New technologies saved time and labor, especially around the house, but these inventions also isolated women in their homes.[10] Women began using new kitchen technologies and gadgets like "iron cookstoves, eggbeaters, and methods for canning and food preservations."[11] Science seemed to be improving everything, so it seemed natural to take a scientific approach to food and cooking.

The domestic science movement of the late nineteenth and early twentieth centuries wasn't only about improving recipes and the taste of recipes but about changing the way families ate.[12] Cooking schools opened to teach domestic science and became popular with women of all economic and social backgrounds. The Boston Cooking School was just one of many domestic science schools to open during this time, but one of its principals, Fannie Farmer, changed the way women cooked at home.

Farmer wrote *The Boston Cooking-School Cook Book* in 1896. In addition to recipes, it included information on nutrition and measurements, and education on food preparation and cooking techniques. Her inclusion of level measurements allowed cooks to create recipes consistent with what the recipe author intended. Farmer also is often credited with creating some of the standard recipe writing formulas still used today. Her recipes follow a format easily recognizable to a modern cook.

GERMAN TOAST

    3 eggs
    ½ teaspoon salt
    2 tablespoons sugar
    I cup milk
    6 slices stale bread

Beat eggs slightly, add salt, sugar, and milk; strain into a shallow dish. Soak bread in mixture until soft. Cook on a hot, well-greased griddle; brown on one side, turn and brown on other side. Serve for breakfast or luncheon, or with a sauce for dessert.[13]

As the twentieth century progressed, new domestic experts, created or sponsored by large corporations, also offered advice to women through radio programs, newspaper columns, and correspondence programs. The most famous was the fictitious Betty Crocker. These experts touted the benefits of electrical appliances and other kitchen technologies, and taught women how to use them. They also marketed new prepackaged foods and food mixes, and provided recipes for using these new types of food.

Some of the most influential cookbooks of the mid-twentieth century were Betty Crocker's *Picture Cook Book*, *The Joy of Cooking* by Irma S. Rombauer and Marion Rombauer Becker, and *Mastering the Art of French Cooking* by Julia Child, Louisette Bertholle, and Simone Beck. Betty Crocker's cookbook contains cooking tips, clear directions, and illustrations to help cooks perform more difficult tasks like preparing a chicken for roasting.[14] *The Joy of Cooking* began as a self-published work written by a mother and daughter and evolved into many editions. The last edition celebrates the seventy-fifth anniversary of the book. Julia Child sought to bring French cooking to American women; her dream resulted in a book, the first cooking show on television, and her place as the precursor of today's celebrity chefs.

COMMUNITY COOKBOOKS

Most people familiar with community cookbooks think of comb-bound volumes, but they can also be hardcover, coil-bound, or even stapled at the spine, all depending on the age and printing method chosen. These community cookbooks gained popularity as fundraisers to help women support causes they valued. While women had limited political and financial means, one way they could contribute to a cause was by submitting recipes to a cookbook that could then be sold to raise money.

The community cookbook, also known as the charity cookbook or fundraising cookbook, first emerged during the American Civil War. *A Poetical Cook-Book* by Maria J. Moss, published in 1864, helped raise funds for the sanitary commission and its work helping Union soldiers. While Moss's book is the first recorded community cookbook, the idea of women contributing to cookbooks was not a new one. Women had always collected recipes from family and friends for their own private manuscript cookbooks. It was just the first time that the idea was transformed into a way to raise funds.[15]

Cookbooks were written to help raise funds for the Presbyterian Church, Methodist Church, Methodist Episcopal Church, Baptist Church, and Episcopal Church as well as the "Brethren Church, Business and Professional Women, Catholic Church, cemetery associations, children's charities, Christ Church, Christian Church, Christian Temperance Union, Confederate Relief, Congregational Church, D.A.R., Dorcas Society, Eastern Star, Epworth League, fairs and expositions, granges, home economics and domestic science organizations, Homes for the Friendless, hospitals, Jewish charities, King's Daughters, libraries, Lutheran Church, Moravian Church, Quaker groups, Reformed Church,

Sanitary Commission..., schools, sororities, Trinity Church, Unitarian Church, United Daughters of the Confederacy, Universalist Church, vegetarian groups, Women's Exchange, Women's Relief Corps and G.A.R., women's suffrage proponents, and YMCA and YWCA."[16]

Since then, community cookbooks have continued to be written and published by groups as varied as church women's organizations and auxiliaries, schools, hospitals, suffrage organizations, community groups, schools and colleges, women's groups, libraries, and historical and genealogical societies.

While most community cookbooks are published once or reprinted a few times, a few became so popular that they served generations of readers. *The Settlement Cook Book*, first published in 1901, was compiled by a committee of women who had been teaching new immigrants the "American way," including how to cook. That book has been updated and republished many times and has sold more than two million copies.[17] While the names of the women are not included with each recipe, names are published on the title page of the original volume.

Although not typically used as a genealogical source, these cookbooks do serve as a resource to place a woman in a particular locality at a specific time. Increasingly, historians are recognizing the value these cookbooks bring to understanding the lives of women. Cookbook expert Janice Bluestein Longone says of these cookbooks, "They also record historical, philosophical, and religious aspects of their compilers and thus of their country."[18]

74

Community cookbooks contain valuable family history information that can help you re-create your ancestor's community. Like many genealogical sources, community cookbooks are at the very least a "names list." They provide a name and a place. Community cookbooks vary on what information can be found in the cookbook. The standard is to have pages of recipes with the name of the woman who submitted each recipe. In earlier cookbooks, that name might include Mrs. and a husband's name or initials, leaving only unmarried women with their full names included. Many cookbooks also include additional information ranging from a photograph of the recipe contributor to family history information explaining the significance of the recipe to the family. Depending on the group organizing the cookbook, you can find occupations, personal histories, and even clues to ethnic backgrounds. Advertisements from local businesses helped offset the printing cost of the cookbook and provide nice details about what was available to your ancestor. These advertisements serve almost as a city directory, allowing you to reconstruct your ancestor's community. Additionally, some cookbooks include information about the group that the book is raising money for. For example, cookbooks produced by church groups may contain church histories, names of ministers, and information on church auxiliaries and missions.

Another reason community cookbooks are so important to researching your family history is they represent food that real people ate. If you have ever donated a recipe to a community cookbook, it was most likely a family favorite or one you thought your friends would enjoy. The same was true for your ancestors. These are recipes that women in the community were proud of and used themselves, recipes they wanted to share with others, recipes that serve as reminders of their lives.

These cookbooks reflect what the families in your ancestor's community really ate. They included ingredients available to their region. Depending on the place and era, hunting or raising small animals may have been the preferred way to obtain protein, especially in difficult financial times. The gathering of rabbits, squirrels, and pigeons, for instance, was an easy and inexpensive way to feed a family. Many of these cookbooks have an underlying theme of feeding families on a budget or with what is available.

These recipes would take into consideration any food restrictions adhered to because of religion. When you are preparing recipes from an ancestor's community cookbook, you will be eating the food they likely ate on a regular basis.

Chapter six provides detailed information on where and how to find community cookbooks.

Your Ancestors Dined Out?

MENUS
Eating out is second nature in modern American culture. A Pew Research study found that a third of Americans eat out less than weekly, a third say they eat out weekly, and the final third say they eat out twice a week or more.[19] While most of us eat out quite frequently, we probably can remember a time when eating out for our family was rare and considered a treat. Although for your own family, eating out may not have been the norm, that doesn't mean that our ancestors never ate out. While restaurants in France in the eighteenth century catered to those in higher classes, early American restaurant food was served in taverns and inns to customers who were often men who were boarders, traveling through, or left to their own

devices. These establishments provided a limited menu and served meals at set times.

Some of the more famous long-standing restaurants are found in New York City. Early residents ate at taverns and even oyster houses, but things changed when Delmonico's opened in 1837. Delmonico's originally opened as a pastry shop in 1827, and evolved into a restaurant after a fire destroyed the block where it was located. The menu from Delmonico's in 1838 was eleven pages long and included French dishes with their English translations. Delmonico's was a departure from other restaurants at this time and, like those early French restaurants, catered to a more exclusive clientele. But the restaurant also was different in how it did business. Diners could dine whenever they wished and didn't have to wait for a set hour, which was the custom for other places serving food such as city hotels and diners. The restaurant became the place to eat in New York City during the nineteenth and early twentieth centuries. Delmonico's became so well-known that other restaurants started using the Delmonico name to cash in on its good reputation.

To get a sense of what other New York restaurants were serving during this time period, consider the September 8, 1856, menu from Congress Hall in Saratoga Springs, New York. The menu consisted of:

Soup
Vermicelli

Fish
Baked Bass, port wine sauce
Lobster

Boiled
Leg of Mutton, caper sauce
Chicken
Corned Beef
Ham

Cold Dishes
Westphalia Ham, glace
Tongue, glace

Entrees
Planquette de Veal aux capers

Roast
Beef

Young Chickens	Lamb, mint sauce
Macaroni a la Neapolitan	Mutton
Ragout of Mutton aux vegetables	Loin of Veal
Eels	
Omelettes	

Vegetables	**Pastry**
Boiled Potatoes	Green Apple Pie
Mashed Potatoes	Peach Pie
Rice	Raspberry Pie
Mashed Turnips	Blackberry Pie
Tomatoes	Tapioca Pudding, Butter Sauce
Cabbage	Ice Cream
Squash	
Onions	**Dessert**
Green Corn	Almonds
	Filberts
	Raisons
	Melons

Beverages were also a part of the meal. This included a large menu of alcoholic drinks.[20]

Genealogist and culinary librarian Christine Crawford-Oppenheimer writes that it "was not until after the Civil War that people began to eat out for pleasure. By the end of the 1800s, most large cities had many restaurants."[21]

As the twentieth century approached, dining choices were enhanced by delis, cafeterias, automats, specialty restaurants featuring one type of food, and department stores.

Restaurant fare changed with the times and economic circumstances. Consider a later New York City menu, printed on the window of the Blossom Restaurant in Manhattan. Menu fare included soup and beans for 5 cents, pigs feet and kraut for 10 cents, and three large pork chops for 30 cents.[22]

In the early twentieth century, Americans started eating out more. As automobile ownership became more widespread, so too did the idea of eating out. Duncan Hines, now known more as a cake mix brand, was a real person whose book *Adventures in Good Eating* was sold to over 900,000 Americans.[23] Hines was a printing salesman, and his frequent travels meant eating out regularly in restaurants throughout the United States. His recommendations initially given to friends and acquaintances grew into a book that included five thousand restaurants in 1946 and was consulted by not only those who bought it but millions of others as well.[24] After World War II, as automobile ownership increased and people used their cars to go to work, travel to see family and friends, and go on family vacations, the need for eating out increased even more.

This transition to eating out more often included the origins of the fast-food industry, one best memorialized in a drive-in restaurant located in San Bernardino, California, that served hamburgers, fries, and milkshakes. Dick and Mark McDonald's restaurant featured car-hop service and 15 cent hamburgers. That restaurant, McDonald's, and a host of other fast-food chains have changed the way Americans eat and how they access inexpensive, fast food.

See chapter six for ways to find menus from your ancestors' eras and hometowns.

78

Notes

» [1] Mary Barile, *Cookbooks Worth Collecting* (Radnor, PA: Wallace-Homestead Book Co., 1994), 22.

» [2] Janet Theophano, *Eat My Words: Reading Women's Lives Through the Cookbooks They Wrote* (New York: Palgrave, 2002), 13.

» [3] Mary Barile, *Cookbooks Worth Collecting* (Radnor, PA: Wallace-Homestead Book Co., 1994), 32.

» [4] Amelia Simmons, *American Cookery, or the Art of Dressing Viands, Fish, Poultry, and Vegetables, and the Best Modes of Making Puff-Pastes, Pies, Tarts, Puddings, Custards, and Preserves, and All Kinds of Cakes, From the Imperial Plumb to Plain Cake, Adapted to This Country, and All Grades of Life* (Albany: Charles R. & George Webster, 1796), 27.

» [5] Christopher Kimball, *Fannie's Last Supper: Re-creating One Amazing Meal From Fannie Farmer's 1896 Cookbook* (New York: Hyperion, 2010), 46.

» [6] Mary Barile, *Cookbooks Worth Collecting* (Radnor, PA: Wallace-Homestead Book Co., 1994), 30.

» [7] Mrs. J. Magie, *Milwaukee Cook Book* (Milwaukee: Riverside Printing Co., 1894), 354.

» [8] Ibid., 354.

» [9] "How to Cook A Husband," *Pacific Monthly IV* (1900): 287.

» [10] Susan Marks, *Finding Betty Crocker: The Secret Life of America's First Lady of Food* (New York: Simon & Schuster, 2005), 12.

» [11] Mary Barile, *Cookbooks Worth Collecting* (Radnor, PA: Wallace-Homestead Book Co., 1994), 38.

» [12] Laura Shapiro, *Perfection Salad: Women and Cooking at the Turn of the Century* (New York: Modern Library, 2001), 8.

» [13] Fannie Merritt Farmer, *The Boston Cooking-School Cook Book* (Boston: Little, Brown and Co., 1896), 69.

» [14] Mary Anna DuSablon, *America's Collectible Cookbooks: The History, the Politics, the Recipes* (Athens: Ohio University Press, 1994), 113.

» [15] Mary Barile, *Cookbooks Worth Collecting* (Radnor, PA: Wallace-Homestead Book Co., 1994), 66.

» [16] Janice Bluestein Longone, "Tried Receipts: An Overview of America's Charitable Cookbooks" in *Recipes for Reading: Community Cookbooks, Stories, Histories*, ed. Anne L. Bower (Amherst, Mass.: University of Massachusetts Press, 1997), 21.

» [17] Michigan State University Libraries, "Feeding America: The Settlement Cook Book," Michigan State University, http://digital.lib.msu.edu/projects/cookbooks/html/books/book_52.cfm (accessed October 12, 2011).

» [18] Janice Bluestein Longone, "Tried Receipts: An Overview of America's Charitable Cookbooks" in *Recipes for Reading: Community Cookbooks, Stories, Histories*, ed. Anne L. Bower (Amherst, Mass.: University of Massachusetts Press, 1997), 28.

» [19] Paul Taylor, Cary Funk, and Peyton Craighill, "Eating More; Enjoying Less," Pew Research Center, http://pewresearch.org/pubs/309/eating-more-enjoying-less (accessed October 12, 2011).

» [20] "Bill of Fare [held by] Congress Hall [at] Saratoga Springs," The New York Public Library Flickr stream, http://www.flickr.com/photos/nypl/3990003689/in/photostream/ (accessed October 12, 2011).

» [21] Christine Crawford-Oppenheimer, "Spice up Your Family History with Menus," *Everton's Genealogical Helper* (December 2001): 18.

» [22] Berenice Abbott, "Blossom Restaurant, 103 Bowery, Manhattan," The New York Public Library Flickr stream, http://www.flickr.com/photos/nypl/3110620430/ (accessed October 12, 2011).

» [23] Phyllis Larsh, "Duncan Hines. He is the traveler's authority on where to eat," *Life*, July 8, 1946, 16–17.

» [24] Ibid.

CHAPTER 6

How to Find Your Ancestors' Recipes

*"Recipes are family stories,
tales of particular places
and personal histories."* –Molly O'Neill

Incorporating food into your family history can be a great way to bring your research to life, to interest current generations and get them excited to learn more about their family. This chapter offers research suggestions to help you learn more about family food history through multiple sources in your own family, including oral history, recipe cards, photographs, and family cookbooks. These resources can help you as you document your family history and tell the story of your family's life. Unfortunately not everyone is lucky enough to have an archive of family recipes and heirlooms. What do you do when there are no older relatives to interview and no recipes or heirlooms have survived? This chapter also shows how to re-create lost or unrecorded food traditions through cookbook collections, menus, and manuscript collections.

As you learn more about the recipes and foods that your ancestors ate, a bit of caution is in order. What was once considered a standard food ingredient may now be known to be dangerous and even poisonous. Before you decide to try out that daffodil salad or that old home remedy, please make sure that you consider the ramifications of ingesting or handling unfamiliar ingredients. Additionally, ingredients in recipes from long ago need to be adjusted for modern tastes, and the cooking of the recipes must be tested in order to be prepared on modern stoves and ovens. Measurements and temperatures were not always standardized. Ingredients such as salt may overpower the recipe.

Part two of this book contains a glossary to help you research antiquated or unfamiliar cooking terms. It also has a measurement conversion chart to help you translate archaic measurements.

Cooking Ephemera

Families often have cooking ephemera associated with different female ancestors. What is cooking ephemera? Ephemera refers to disposable paper items originally meant for short-term (in many cases single) use. They weren't meant to be saved or archived. Examples include greeting cards, invitations, newspapers, letters, postcards, and maps. Food-related ephemera includes menus, cooking pamphlets, articles torn out of newspapers, and recipe cards. Cooking ephemera allows us to re-create a traditional recipe, learn more about the recipes of our ancestor's time, remember favorite restaurants, and even get a look at a different place and time.

One of the problems with ephemera is that it's often printed on poor-quality paper that doesn't stand up to the test of time. Acids found in the paper cause it to deteriorate. This is what causes newspaper to yellow and become brittle. Because the paper becomes so fragile, it's important to take steps to ensure that your family ephemera will be preserved for future generations. These steps include proper storage and handling. Heirlooms like the same conditions that we like—not too hot or too cold, not too humid or too dry, away from direct sunlight. They last longer when they are not handled too often because oils from our hands can transfer onto the paper item and cause damage.

As you preserve ephemera, consider what is the best way to archive the item and still let family members have access to it. It's almost impossible to reverse damage on a piece of ephemera, so it's important to stabilize the object to prevent any future damage. Consider scanning these items so you have a digitized copy that can be shared. This will allow all family members to "own" the item and display, share, and use it without endangering the original.

Never use a laminator or any other method that cannot be undone. For many years, people believed that lamination preserved items, but it actually doesn't stop the deterioration, and it can never be undone. Use archival-safe products to store the item, including page protectors, albums, and boxes. Archival-safe products can be found at scrapbooking stores, library/museum suppliers, and other online vendors.

Home Sources

As with any genealogical research project, it's vital to start with what you know and search for home sources that you have access to. A home source is an item of genealogical significance that a person has in his or her house. Typically in family history research, we think of items such as family Bibles, photographs, correspondence, passports, vital record certificates, newspaper clippings and yearbooks—basically anything that has a family member's name and other identifying information. These items help us create a timeline for the ancestor's life and place the person in a specific time and locality. Home sources are often thought of as documents and heirlooms housed in a researcher's own home, but this definition is too limited as we try to re-create our family's food traditions.

With family food traditions, the best approach is to ask different members of the family for any material they may own. Ask about any cookbooks and recipes they have that have been handed down through the family, and ask what heirlooms they have inherited that were involved in the preparation and presentation of food in your family. Kitchen tools, furniture, appliances, tablecloths and linens, aprons, silverware, pottery, and china all help tell the story of your family. Also, don't forget any photographs of the family's kitchen, holidays, celebrations, or family members preparing food. These photographs can provide valuable clues about meals, meal preparation, and family. Photos of family seated around the table will bring back memories of the smells, the food, and the traditions.

You can use these photos to add interest to a family history narrative or to add images to a family history cookbook. Ask family members to scan photos and ephemera for you and share them via e-mail. Or, if you are visiting a family member, bring a small or portable scanner to scan photos, recipes, small heirlooms, and documents so you don't have to borrow the items. People are often hesitant to let family heirlooms out of their sight. By bringing your own scanner you increase your possibility of obtaining copies of these items. Make sure to use a flatbed scanner to avoid damaging any of the items you are scanning. Once you are done scanning items, you can burn the digitized images to a CD, transfer image files to a portable drive, have copies made at a photo processor, or upload them to an online photo- or file-sharing site so other family members can have access to those image files.

Interviews

As you gather home sources from other family members, ask them to share their memories. You can contact family members through e-mail correspondence or through social networking sites such as Facebook where you can conduct a private chat or send a private message to a group of family members. Sending a message to a group of people allows family members to read each other's responses, which may help trigger more memories in each person. This is a great way to solicit memories from the younger generations in your family. While you may have specific food memories about your grandmother, your cousin's memories offer a different perspective and could add to what you already know. For example every summer my family visited my maternal grandmother and stayed with her for a few weeks. Inevitably one of the foods we enjoyed while there was watermelon. A cousin later told me that my grandmother had warned him as a small child that if he swallowed any watermelon seeds, the fruit would grow in his stomach. (I believe this was probably an effort on her part to make him behave.) He feared eating watermelon because of the potential fruit that would take over his stomach. Now something as everyday as eating watermelon reminds me of my cousin who grew up believing that he was destined to have a watermelon grow inside himself.

To collect the memories of older generations you will probably need to set up oral interviews. These interviews can be short discussions conducted either in person or over the phone. Be respectful of the person's time and limit the length of your interview. It's better to conduct a few separate, short sessions than to wear the person out with endless questions. Sometimes as family historians we get so excited about learning new information that we forget not everyone is as excited with the research process.

Whether you conduct your interview over the internet, over the phone, or in person, realize that when you initially ask questions, people tend to

*From
the
Family
Kitchen*

83

PART i
CH. 6

say that they don't remember, that they have no memories of a specific subject, or that their stories aren't important. Assure them that anything they can share is valuable, and give them time to reflect on each question.

You may even consider providing them with the questions ahead of time to give them an opportunity to ponder each one. Most important, really listen to what the person is saying. Ask open-ended questions that require more than a yes or no answer.

INTERVIEW QUESTIONS

To help you get started with questions to ask, I've included the following interview questions, but don't limit yourself to just these. As the person tells his or her story, you'll likely think of additional follow-up questions. Don't be afraid to ask these. It's important to see where the interview leads you and not be too rigid.

Some questions you can include in your interview are:

Family History

» What did you eat as a child?
» What did you eat at your grandparents' house?
» What did the older people in the family eat? (Sometimes this can be different than what the children were willing to eat.)
» Did you eat anything then that your family would not be willing to eat now?
» What was your favorite meal growing up?
» How did you learn to cook? Who taught you?
» What was the first meal you prepared?
» How was food different when you married?
» What did your in-laws serve that was different? What were their food traditions?
» Was any of the food you ate handed down from immigrant ancestors? If you were the immigrant, what foods did you continue to prepare once in the United States? What ingredients were difficult to find? Did you change the recipe at all?
» Who was the best cook in the family? Why? What did they prepare?
» What kinds of desserts did you eat? Did you have a favorite?

When asking the questions above, make sure to ask about biographical information (birth date/place, death date/place, spouse information, how the person was related) for any relatives you may be unfamiliar with. Add that information to your genealogy database program.

Food Production

» Where did your family get most of the food you ate—grocery store, farm, small garden, hunting, fishing, gathering, bartering?

» Did you or a family member work in a profession associated with food, like farming?

» If you grew a garden, what produce did you grow?

» How did you use the produce—to feed your family, to sell to or barter with others, to feed livestock?

» How did you prepare produce grown for your family to eat?

» If you lived during World War II, did you plant a victory garden?

» If you raised chickens, what did you do with the eggs? Whose job was it to gather them? Did you ever candle an egg?

» What kinds of meat did you eat? Was the meat mostly store-bought or did you raise or hunt animals?

» Did you take care of any animals that were used to produce food for your family (e.g., milking cows or goats, feeding chickens, raising rabbits)?

» How did you preserve food? Did you can? Did you dehydrate food? Did you have an icebox?

Kitchens

» What memories do you have of your parents' or grandparents' kitchen?

» What kind of kitchen tools did they use? Did those get passed down?

» What appliances did your grandparents and parents have in their kitchens?

» What, if any, appliances were added to the kitchen of your childhood home (e.g., refrigerator, gas range, toaster over, ice cream maker)?

» How did these new appliances change how your mother or father prepared food?

» How did new appliances change the types of foods you ate?

» What, if any, appliances did you add to your kitchen as an adult (e.g., dishwasher, microwave)?

» How did these new appliances change how you prepared food? How did they change the foods you ate?

Meals During Certain Historical Eras

» How were meals different in hard times (i.e., the Great Depression, World War II, maybe a time when a family member lost his or her job, crops failed, etc.)?

*From
the
Family
Kitchen*

85

PART I
CH. 6

» If you lived during World War II, what do you remember about rationing? How did that affect what you ate? How did your family use food substitutes and modify favorite recipes? Did you save any of the ration coupons?

Cookbooks

» What cookbooks did your family use?

» Did you or anyone in the family contribute to a community cookbook? If so, who created the cookbook, and whom did it benefit? What recipe or recipes did you submit? Why did you select that recipe? Do you have a copy of the cookbook?

» Do you or does another family member have a recipe box? Where are those recipes now?

» What was the first cookbook you owned? What dishes did you cook from it that you enjoyed?

» What were some favorite recipes you found in a cookbook?

Dining Out

» How often did your family eat at restaurants?

» When or why would your family eat at a restaurant (e.g., special occasions, when traveling, to take a break from cooking, family vacations, or for no special reason at all)?

» If you can remember any of the restaurant names, what were they and where were they located? What types of food did you eat there?

RECORDING INTERVIEWS

There are many options available to help you record your oral interviews. I've listed the most common below. When deciding on your recording method, make sure the person you are interviewing is comfortable with the type of recording you choose.

Audio Cassette Recording

A tape cassette or microcassette player/recorder lets you record and play back what you have recorded. If you are conducting several interviews, you may want to invest in a cassette transcriber, which allows you to start and stop the recording with a foot pedal control. This keeps your hands free so you can keep your fingers on your computer keyboard and quickly transcribe the recording. Cassette transcribers are relatively expensive compared to regular players/recorders, but they can make transcribing your hours of interviews much easier. Also consider using an external microphone for the best sound quality.

Digital Audio Recording

Digital audio recorders are similar to cassette recorders except they allow you to record and then download the recording to your computer via a USB cable. The benefit of this is the ability to store your recordings on your computer and listen to them from your computer or MP3 players. You can also easily share these audio files by e-mailing them to other family members. Digital recorders are available at electronics stores and office supply stores. You may also want to purchase a microphone to improve the sound quality.

Video Recording

Some people prefer to video record their interviews so they have an image to go with their sound. These video recordings, depending on the recorder you purchase, can then be uploaded, edited, and copied on your computer. The benefit of a video recording is obvious: You can watch the person tell his or her life story. The drawback is that not everyone is comfortable being video recorded, so the person you are interviewing may be hesitant to answer questions. Videotaping an interview is much more intrusive than using a small, inconspicuous audio recording device.

Skype Recording

New technology makes it possible to record interviews with family members even if they live a hundred or even thousands of miles away. Skype <www.skype.com> is a free telephone service that allows you to call anyone in the world through the internet. Free calls must be made computer-to-computer, and each person on the call must have a Skype account. Your computer must have a microphone and speakers so you can hear the call and speak to the person on the other end. The Skype Recording app <http://web2oeducation.amplify.com> lets you record Skype calls. Other apps that can record Skype calls include CallBurner and SkyLook. This is a great option for interviewing family members who live far away.

TRANSCRIBING INTERVIEWS

When selecting a recording method, remember you will need to transcribe the information, so consider which method will make it easiest for you to transcribe and share the information. Don't wait to transcribe your interviews. If you wait too long, you may find your recording technology is obsolete. Nothing is worse than spending a lot of time on a project, letting it sit for a while, and then realizing that the equipment you have no longer works and there is no replacement.

After you transcribe the material, have the person you interviewed review what you have written. Make sure they are comfortable with what will be shared. Sometimes, in an effort to tell an interesting story, people can make statements they later regret. Also use this time to follow up on questions that may have come to you when reading over the interview. If the person talked about a favorite recipe, ask if you can get a copy. Ask for permission to take photos of any heirlooms related to your family's food history. After you've transcribed the interview and it has been reviewed, you can incorporate these remembrances into a family cookbook, wiki, blog, or a family history book.

Searching Your Past Online

Always start your research with home sources. After you've exhausted those, turn your search to outside sources. As with any family history project, looking for answers through an internet search engine such as Google may be a good way to begin. You can find additional information on the history of family recipes, search for relevant cookbooks, and more.

A search engine is like a card catalog system for the internet. And just like a card catalog, it may take multiple searches using different keywords and variant spellings to find what you are looking for. Popular search engines include Bing <bing.com>, Google <google.com>, and Yahoo <yahoo.com>.

With any search engine, the more keywords you include, the fewer results you will receive. This can be a good and bad thing. With genealogy searches of a common surname like Smith, narrowing a search can help focus the search on the person or region you are researching. However, remember with search engines, the way you have typed a search is exactly how the search engine will look for it. The search engine is not able to ascertain that A.K. Smith and Alice K. Smith are the same person. This is why conducting numerous searches with variations on a name can yield more pertinent results. In Google, to receive more precise results, place your search term or phrase in quotation marks. This tells the Google search engine that you want to search on an exact phrase. For example, if you are searching for recipes for mincemeat pie, placing the phrase in quotations will give you results that contain those two words together instead of websites that have the word *mincemeat* and the word *pie* somewhere on the page, but not necessarily together. So instead of searching on *mince-meat pie* and getting over two million results, you would search *"mincemeat pie"* and get a little over 250,000. Just remember that exact phrase searching does have drawbacks. When you search an exact phrase, Google will only look for that phrase. So a search for *"Alice Smith"* will not find *"Alice K. Smith."* A search for *"mince pie"* will not find *"mincemeat pie."*

The Advanced Search link on any search engine is another way to narrow your search. The advanced search lets you take a keyword or phrase and find web pages that contain a series of words or an exact phrase. You can also indicate that certain words not show up on the webpage. This is a great tool to use when searching a common surname (e.g., Smith, Jones) and surnames that could be used as in another context (e.g., Young, Few). I'm researching the surname *Chatham,* which is also a common county name in several southern states. To ensure my search results don't include sites for Chatham counties, I click on Advanced search and exclude *county* and any other unwanted word in my search. If you were researching an ancestor named Benjamin Smith and received page after page of results for a Benjamin Smith in Virginia, but your Benjamin Smith lived in Minnesota, you could exclude *Virginia* from your search to eliminate unrelated results.

In Google, Advanced search also lets you determine results by reading level, language of the websites, and file format (for specifying formats like PDFs, PowerPoint slides, and Microsoft Word docs). The other great thing about the Advanced search is that you can use it not only to search the entire internet but also to search just one website. From the Google home page, click on the Gear icon, located at the top right of the screen. Then click on Advance search. In the Advanced search box, under the heading "Need more tools?" enter the URL of the site you want to search in the box labeled "Search within a site or domain."

Additional tools include how recent the page is, usage rights, where the keywords show up on the web page, region, and numeric range.

Google

Google has a number of search options that are very helpful to genealogists. This section highlights some of them. You can find all of the searches mentioned in this section plus other Google searches by going to the Google Products page at <www.google.com/prdhp>. It's important to know that Google is always making improvements and enhancements to its websites. Because of this, directions found in this book for using Google may change over time. You can learn more about changes to Google by consulting the official Google blog <http://googleblog.blogspot.com/>.

Family Tree University <familytreeuniversity.com> also offers a number of courses and webinars that can teach you even more about using Google in your research, including Google Tools for Genealogists and Advanced Google for Genealogists.

GOOGLE NEWS ARCHIVE

Google News Archive <news.google.com/archivesearch> provides a one-stop place to search for newspapers. As of the writing of this book, Google had announced that it would not be adding to Google News Archive, but the newspapers that have been digitized through that project will continue to be available there.

To search the Google News Archive, go to <http://news.google.com/archivesearch>. Type your keywords into the appropriate boxes under the Find results heading. Under the Date heading, select Return articles added to Google News Archive. You can narrow the dates of the results using filters on the left side of the Results page.

Your search results will provide you a little bit of information about the context of the article, just as any Google search results show. It will also provide you with a link to the article and tell you if there is a cost to view the article. In some cases, these are articles digitized by Google, and in other cases, they are from various newspapers and other websites, so there may be a nominal cost to access the article. Click on the free results to view them on a different Google page.

You can't save or download the articles in the Google News Archive, but you can save a link to the article. Click Link to Article in the top right corner of the article page. I have also used a screen shot program to save a copy of the article to my computer.

GOOGLE TIMELINE

After you conduct a search and are looking at your search results, you can view those results in different ways. One way is to utilize the Timeline View. To do this, click on Timeline, located on the left-hand menu under the heading More Search Tools>All Results. Google will sort your results according to date from the earliest to the latest. The date that is used is the date mentioned in the article, not the date the information was posted to the internet. A timeline at the top of the list allows you to click on a time period and go straight to those results. How can the Timeline View improve your search results? Say you are researching an ancestor who lived around 1860, but a later descendent has the same name. By using the Timeline view you can narrow your search by the time period for the ancestor you are looking for instead of the latter descendent. If you are searching a recipe, you can use the Timeline View to narrow the time period for the recipe. A mincemeat pie recipe published now can be very different from a mincemeat pie recipe from the late 1800s.

You can easily close out of the Timeline View by clicking on the X at the top right of the Timeline screen. This will return you to the results list.

GOOGLE BOOKS

Google Books <books.google.com/books> houses millions of books and periodicals from libraries and publishers. The books on Google Books run the gamut of classics and children's literature, fiction and nonfiction titles as well as magazines from the 1800s to the present day. You can also find county histories, published genealogies, and rare and out-of-print books. All types of cookbooks are represented on Google Books, from the latest, most popular cookbooks authored by celebrity chefs to church cookbooks from the 1890s. Books fall into four viewing options, depending on their copyright restrictions: Full Preview, Limited Preview, Snippet View, and No Preview Available.

Full Preview means you can view the entire content of the book on Google. These books are either no longer copyright protected and are in the public domain, or the author or publisher has given permission for the book to be fully digitized on Google Books. If the book is in the public domain, it is available for downloading to your computer or mobile device such as iPad, iPod, Nook, and Android device. You can also save or print the book as a PDF.

Books that are newer and covered by copyright protection are only available for Limited Preview, a Snippet View, or No Preview. Limited Preview shows a certain number of pages from a book, and as you browse the book, you will notice that some pages are missing. Google compares the Snippet View to a library card catalog, but it shows views of sentences that include your search term. In No Preview, you'll see Google's "card catalog" information but no text from the book.

The "Get this book" link in a search result will take you to a results page containing links to online booksellers who have that specific title available for sale. A link for "Find in a library" will take you to that book's page on the WorldCat website. If you're not familiar with WorldCat, it is an online library catalog that searches more than 10,000 libraries and 1.5 billion items, including books, periodicals, archival materials, theses and dissertations, and other resources.

Search Google Books exactly as you would any search engine. Google Books, like all Google searches, includes an Advanced search link where you can narrow your search, based on publisher, title, language, author, subject, and publication date.

GOOGLE BLOG SEARCH

Google Blog Search <google.com/blogsearch> can assist you as you search for others who are writing about food and family history. Google Blog Search is a specialized search just for blogs. It has a similar look and feel to the Google search engine. Filters for narrowing your search can be found on the left-hand side of the results page. If you want to narrow your search to blogs that have been updated more recently, you can do that by clicking on the heading "Sorted by relevance" and then clicking "Sorted by date."

FINDING COMMUNITY COOKBOOKS

Chapter five details all of the valuable information you can find in a community cookbook. While many repositories have viewed community cookbooks as items not worthy of long-term, or even short-term, archiving, there are ways to find community cookbooks that document the locality you are researching, and you may even find one that includes a listing of a family member's name.

As with any research, first begin with the homes of family members. Ask them to search in their collections of cookbooks and books for any community cookbooks that mention family members or are from the community or church your family was a part of.

As you broaden your search, consider checking available bibliographies, archival and library collections, digitized book sites, and online auction websites. If you are in the area where your ancestor lived, you can expand your search to local library collections, used bookstores, friends of the library book sales, and thrift stores. Also check with churches or clubs your ancestor may have been a member of. Copies might be found with current members or in the archives.

A few bibliographies do exist of community cookbooks, including *America's Charitable Cooks* by Margaret Cook and *Canadian Culinary Landmarks* by

Elizabeth Driver. These will give you a foundation for finding community cookbooks published during specific time periods.

LIBRARIES

A few American libraries house large collections of community cookbooks including:

» Los Angeles Public Library
   <www.lapl.org/resources/guides/food_drink.html>
» William L. Clements Library at the University of Michigan
   <www.clements.umich.edu/longone-archive.php>
» University of Illinois Library
   <www.library.illinois.edu/learn/exhibit/index.htm>
» The Library of Congress
   <www.loc.gov/rr/scitech/SciRefGuides/americancookbooks.html>
» The Radcliffe Institute, Harvard University, Schlesinger Library
   <www.radcliffe.edu/schles/taste.aspx>
» Rutgers University Libraries <www.libraries.rutgers.edu/rul/libs/scua/
   sinclair/sinclair_cook_books_main.shtml>
» University of Massachusetts Amherst
   <www.library.umass.edu/spcoll/cookbooks/?page_id=202>

To find other libraries that may assist you in your search, consult the website Libraries in the United States <www.librarysites.info/>.

You can begin your library search by using WorldCat <www.worldcat. org>, a union catalog of libraries with over 1.5 billion items available to search. WorldCat includes library catalogs from throughout the world, but not all libraries participate in WorldCat. Additionally, the WorldCat website available to the general public is smaller than the one available to librarians as they look for repositories for patrons' interlibrary loan requests.

When searching for a community cookbook in a library catalog, it is important to go beyond using a keyword to searching by a subject heading. Subject headings are categories that librarians use to catalog books.

In the case of cookbooks, the subject heading has historically been *cookery,* not *cookbooks*. While this was changed recently, you may still find cookbooks using that subject heading. You may also want to try other keywords like *church cookbook* as well as the name of the locality your ancestor lived in. A reference librarian can assist you and suggest other keywords and subject headings that may yield more results.

DIGITIZED BOOK WEBSITES

Digitized book websites provide genealogists with a convenient way to peruse new and old books online. These sites provide access to community cookbooks, although they are not categorized in that way. A careful search of digitized book websites will reveal cookbooks listed under various categories that can be found by searching on keywords like the locality your ancestors lived in, the church they attended, or the social group they belonged to.

Older books, typically those published prior to 1923, are usually in the public domain, and websites will digitize the entire text for you to peruse. You can use images and recipes from books in the public domain to illustrate a family history. Digitized books with limited previews have certain copyright restrictions that you want to be aware of. Don't copy material from these books for your family history because the content is still protected by copyright laws. Make sure you obtain permission to use materials found in a book.

Google Books is an example of a digitized book website. Another site worth searching for community cookbooks is the Internet Archive's text collection, which has a sub-collection entitled Cooking <www.archive.org/details/cbk>. This collection includes books from the libraries at UCLA, UC Berkeley, and the Prelinger Library. You can search this collection by title or by author. A browse by subject feature is available; however, it lists only one community cookbook, even though there are many more that are not listed by that subject. The best way to search this collection is mostly by title, paying special attention to those titles that name a locality, church, or organization.

ONLINE AUCTIONS

While a library or archive in your ancestors' locality might hold the promise of a collection of community cookbooks or menus, another place to search is an internet auction site like eBay. EBay as a genealogical source? Of course! EBay is a source for finding thousands of items of historical and genealogical value, including correspondence, photographs, and family Bibles. Menus and community cookbooks that run the gamut of church, school, and organizational books spanning the nineteenth and twentieth centuries can be found in large numbers on eBay.

When searching on eBay, make sure to try various keywords so your search can be as comprehensive as possible. Some search terms to try include *community cookbook, church cookbooks,* or *fundraising cookbooks.* You can also specify a type of cookbook in your search like *Grange Cookbook* or *Methodist Cookbook*. EBay will also suggest other keywords that you can click on. Also consider creating an alert that will notify you when an item related to an ancestor's locality, church, membership organization, or a cookbook comes up for sale.

MANUSCRIPT COLLECTIONS

Manuscript collections bring richness and depth to your understanding of your ancestors' world. They provide the context and background to all those dates and places family historians normally are busily collecting. Manuscript collections go beyond the genealogy staples of census records, military records, and vital records. They are the documents and personal papers of everyday life.

A manuscript collection, sometimes referred to as a special collection, is, by definition, the unpublished papers of a person, group, or organization. But, in reality, manuscript collections can include so much more than just documents. They may include theses or dissertations, photograph albums, ephemera, letters, diaries or journals, business documents, scrapbooks, birthday and autograph books, vital record substitutes, maps, court records, an author's research notes, correspondence, and more, including handwritten cookbooks, menus, and recipe collections.

Manuscripts may be from a government entity or official, a business, a nonprofit group, a religious organization, a society, an institution, a membership group, or an individual. They may be located at a public, private, state, or university library as well as a county, state, or organization archive or historical/genealogical society or museum.

There are two important things to remember when researching a manuscript collection. First, don't search by an ancestor's surname alone. You want to look for manuscripts that deal with your ancestor's locality, community, neighbors, religion, or occupation. Your ancestor's writings may not have been left to a library, but the journal of someone who lived in his or her community or the recipes collected from the local church that were never published in a cookbook may have been. If you limit your search to only your ancestor, you may miss other collections that can help you.

Second, collections usually contain finding aids that help you better understand and search the individual collection. Don't conduct just a keyword or subject search like you would for a genealogy subscription website. Consult the collection's finding aid, or ask an archivist or reference librarian for information about the collection and its contents.

Manuscript collections are unpublished works that are one of a kind, so they must be handled and stored carefully. Archives that hold manuscript collections may have special rules about their use to protect the collections. These rules may dictate how and if items can be handled or copied as well as what collections are available to the general public. Make sure you consult the library or archive website for any rules or ask the librarian or archivist in charge of the collection before making a trip to the repository.

There are various ways to find manuscripts and special collections. One method is searching on the National Union Catalog of Manuscript Collections (NUCMC) <www.loc.gov/coll/nucmc>. While NUCMC's catalog is not a comprehensive source, it is a good place to start. You can search NUCMC by subject, surname, or locality. Hits will provide you with the name of the item and where it is located. After you have that information, consult that repository's library or special collections catalog for more information.

Another option for finding manuscript collections is by using a collaborative library/archive catalog like the Online Archive of California <www.oac.cdlib.org> or the Mountain West Digital Library <mwdl.org>.

Also search online card catalogs for state archives or libraries, historical and genealogical societies, and museums.

In some cases, manuscript collections might be digitized and available online, or they may be microfilmed, but typically these collections must be viewed on site. If you are unable to travel to the collection's location, you may want to consider hiring a local researcher to search the collection for you.

You can find researchers by consulting the websites of the Association of Professional Genealogists <www.apgen.org>, the Board for Certification of Genealogists <www.bcgcertification.org>, and the International Commission for the Accreditation of Professional Genealogists <www.icapgen.org/icapgen>.

In the case where a collection is housed at a university library, you may be able to find a student who can make copies for you at a nominal charge.

Additional websites that might assist you in finding collections include Archives & Manuscript Collections <library.columbia.edu/eguides/archives_manuscript.html> and the Repositories of Primary Sources <www.uiweb.uidaho.edu/special-collections/Other.Repositories.html>.

The Periodical Source Index (PERSI)

PERSI is compiled by the Allen County Public Library in Fort Wayne, Indiana. With 1.7 million articles in 6,000 different periodicals, PERSI is the largest index of historical and genealogical articles in the world. This index covers articles written in English and French since 1800. Articles in PERSI include historical pieces as well as transcriptions of documents, cemeteries, and books. A search on a locality may include results such as the names of recipe contributors or advertisers transcribed from a community cookbook.

While you cannot access PERSI from the Allen County Public Library website, you can access it through paid subscription sites Ancestry.com <www.ancestry.com> or Heritage Quest Online <www.heritagequeston-line.com>. To search PERSI through Ancestry, go to the Ancestry home page and click on the Search tab. If you scroll down, on the right-hand side of the page there is a list of databases. Under the heading Reference, Dictionaries and Almanacs look for PERSI.

Heritage Quest is available at some public libraries. Consult your local library's website or ask a librarian to see if they have a subscription to Heritage Quest. Libraries that subscribe to Heritage Quest often allow users access to the site from their home computer with their library card.

You can search PERSI by locality, surname, or keyword. PERSI is indexed by the title of the article, not the content in the article, so it's a good idea to search locality and keyword. By just conducting a surname search, you could miss out on important data.

When you search by locality, you will be rewarded with everything from transcriptions of community cookbooks, recipes, and histories of towns and cities, to cemetery transcriptions, directories, and pioneer-family histories. When you search by locality, you can also add a keyword to help narrow your search.

After you have searched PERSI and found the articles you are interested in, you can download an order form from the Allen County Public Library website at <http://www.genealogycenter.org/pdf/ArticleRequest.pdf>. You can also get a copy of this form from the Ancestry website. For the order form, you will need the title of the article, name of the journal, volume number, month, and year. The cost to order articles is $7.50 per order, up to six articles per order form. Allen County will charge you 20 cents per page for photocopying. You can expect to receive your photo-copied articles in six to eight weeks.

MENU COLLECTIONS

Restaurants in America began as food served in taverns and inns to mostly a male clientele, but then grew in the nineteenth century to be the establishments we are accustomed to today. While not all of our ancestors had the money to eat at restaurants, they still may have enjoyed a meal out while traveling or for a special occasion. According to Christine Crawford-Oppenheimer, "The first surviving early menus in America are from the 1840s..."[1] Looking at menus from a different time provides us with an idea of what food may have been available to eat, what people were eating, and what prices they were paying.

The following menu collections include digitized items as well as undigitized archived materials:

» Los Angeles Public Library Menu Collection
  <www.lapl.org/resources/en/menu_collection.html>
» New York Public Library Menu Collection
  <http://legacy.www.nypl.org/research/chss/grd/resguides/menus/index.html>
» New York Public Library Digital Menu Collection
  <http://digitalgallery.nypl.org/nypldigital/explore/dgexplore.cfm?col_id=159>
» University of Washington Menus Collection
  <http://content.lib.washington.edu/menusweb/index.html>
» The Nestlé Library at Cornell University Menus Database
  <www.hotelschool.cornell.edu/research/library/collections/menus>
» Menus: The Art of Dining from the University of Nevada Las Vegas
  <http://digital.library.unlv.edu/collections/menus>
» The Culinary Institute of America Menu Collections
  <www.ciachef.edu/newyork/library/menus.asp>
» Alice Statler Library, City College of San Francisco, Menu Collection
  <www.ccsf.edu/Library/alice/menucollection.html>
» Jane Adams Recipe and Menu Collection, San Diego State University
  <http://dsc.calstate.edu/1665?r=cam>
» New-York Historical Society
  <https://www.nyhistory.org/web/default.php?section=library&page=collections>
» Texas Woman's University Cookbook Collection
  <www.twu.edu/library/cookbook-collection.asp>

While researching your family's food history is slightly different than the traditional genealogical search that involves looking up government records and documents online and at libraries and archives, the effort will pay out with the addition of social history that brings your ancestors' past to life.

Notes

» [1] Christine Crawford-Oppenheimer, "Spice up Your Family History With Menus," *Everton's Genealogical Helper* (December 2001): 19.

PART

2

A Look Back at

Historical Recipes

CHAPTER 7

Decipher Old Cooking Terms

102

As you discover old recipes, you may notice they either lack measurements for the ingredients or they employ measuring standards no longer used. You also might find unfamiliar cooking terms. This chapter contains a glossary of cooking terms from *The Boston Cooking-School Cook Book* by Fannie Farmer published in 1896. You'll also find a chart to help you translate or convert some old measurement standards.

COOKING TERMS

Accolade de perdreaux. Brace of partridge.

Agneau. Lamb.

Agra dolce (sour sweet). An Italian sauce served with meat.

À la, au, aux. With or dressed in a certain style.

Allemande (à la). In German style.

Ambrosia. Food for the gods. Often applied to a fruit salad.

Américaine (à l'). In American style.

Ancienne (à l'). In old style.

Angelica. A plant, the stalks of which are preserved and used for decorating moulds.

Asperge. Asparagus.

Au gratin. With browned crumbs.

Aurora sauce. A white sauce to which lobster butter is added.

Avena. Oats.

Axafetida. A gum resin. Its taste is bitter and sub-acrid, and by the Asiatics [sic] it is used regularly as a condiment.

Baba Cakes. Cakes baked in small moulds; made from a yeast dough mixture to which is added butter, sugar, eggs, raisins, and almonds. Served as a pudding with hot sauce.

Bain-Marie. A vessel of any kind containing heated water, in which other vessels are placed in order to keep their contents heated.

Bannocks. Scottish cakes made of barley or oatmeal, cooked on a griddle.

Bards. Slices of pork or bacon to lay on the breast of game for cooking.

Basil. A pot herb.

Bay leaves. Leaves from a species of laurel.

Béarnaise (à la). In Swiss style.

Béarnaise saner. Named from Béarnaise, Swiss home of Henry VIII.

Béchamel (à la). With sauce made of chicken stock and milk or cream.

Beignet. Fritter.

Beurre noir. Black butter.

Biscuit glace. Small cakes of ice cream.

Bisque. A soup usually made from shellfish; or an ice cream to which are added finely chopped nuts.

Blanch (to). To whiten.

Blanquette. White meat in cream sauce.

Boeuf à la jardinière. Braised beef with vegetables.

Boeuf braisé. Braised beef.

Bombe glacée. Moulded ice cream and ice, or two kinds of ice cream. Outside of one kind, filling of another.

Bouchées. Literally, mouthful. Small patties.

Bouquet of herbs. A sprig each of thyme, savory, marjoram, and parsley.

Bourgeoise (à la). In family style.

Bretonne sauce. A stock sauce in which chopped parsley is served.

*From
the
Family
Kitchen*

103

PART 2
CH. 7

Café noir. Black coffee.

Cerrevelles de reau. Calf's brains.

Chartreuse. A mould of aspic in which there are vegetables; a meat preparation filling the centre of the mould. Used to denote anything concealed.

Chateaubriand. A cut from the centre of a fillet of beef.

Chaud-froid. Literally hot cold. In cookery a jellied sauce.

Chou-fleur. Cauliflower.

Chutney. An East India sweet pickle.

Civet. A game stew.

Compotes. Fruits stewed in syrup and kept in original shape.

Con-sommé de volatile. Chicken soup.

Côtelettes. Cutlets.

Court bouillon. A highly seasoned liquor in which to cook fish.

Créole (à la). With tomatoes.

Croûte au pot. A brown soup poured over small pieces of toast.

Curry powder. A yellow powder of which the principal ingredient is turmeric. Used largely in India.

De, d'. Of.

Devilled. Highly seasoned.

Dinde farcie. Stuffed turkey.

Dinde, sauce céleri. Turkey with celery sauce.

Écossaise (à l'). In Scottish style.

En bellevue. In aspic jelly. Applied to meats.

En coquilles. In shells.

En papillotes. In papers.

Éperlans frits. Fried smelts.

Espagnole sauce. A rich brown sauce.

Farci-e. Stuffed.

Fillet de boeuf piqué. Larded fillet of beef.

Flamande (à la). In Holland style.

Foie de veay grillé. Broiled liver.

Fondue. A dish prepared of cheese and eggs.

Fraises. Strawberries.

Frappé. Semi-frozen.

Fricassée de poulet. Fricassee of chicken.

Fromage. Cheese.

Gâteau. Cake.
Gelée. Jelly.
Génevoise (à la). In Swiss style.
Glacé. Iced or glossed over.
Grilled. Broiled.

Hachis de boeuf. Beef hash.
Hoe cakes. Cakes made of white cornmeal, salt, and boiling water; cooked on a griddle.
Homard. Lobster.
Hors—d'oeuvres. Side dishes.
Huîtres en coquille. Oysters in shell.
Huîtres frites. Fried oysters.

Italienne (à l'). In Italian style.

Jambon froid. Cold ham.
Jardiniére. Mixed vegetables.

Kirschwasser. Liqueur made from cherry juice.
Kuchen. German for cake.
Kümmel. Liqueur flavored with cumin and caraway seed.

Lait. Milk.
Laitue. Lettuce.
Langue de boeuf à l'écarlate. Pickled tongue.

Macaroni au fromage. Macaroni with cheese.
Macédoine. A mixture of several kinds of vegetables.
Maigre. A vegetable soup without stock.
Maître d'hôtel. Head steward.
Mango. A fruit of the West Indies, Florida, and Mexico.
Mango pickles. Stuffed and pickled young melons and cucumbers.
Maraschino. A cordial.
Marrons. Chestnuts.
Menu. A bill of fare.
Morue. Salt cod.

Noël. Christmas.

Noir. Black.

Nouilles. Noodles.

Noyau. A cordial.

Oeufs farcis. Stuffed eggs.

Oeufs pochés. Poached eggs.

Omelette aux champignons. Omelette with mushrooms.

Omelette aux fines heroes. Omelette with fine herbs.

Pain. Bread.

Panade. Bread and milk cooked to a paste.

Paté de biftecks. Beefsteak pie.

Paté de foie gras. A paste made of fatted geese livers.

Pigeonneaux. Squabs (young pigeons).

Pois. Peas.

Pommes. Apples.

Pommes de terre. Potatoes.

Pommes de terre à la Lyonnaise. Lyonnaise potatoes.

Pone cakes. A cake made in the South, baked in the oven.

Potage. Soup.

Poulets sautés. Fried chicken.

Queues de boeuf. Ox-tails.

Ragoût. A highly seasoned meat dish.

Réchauffés. Warmed over dishes.

Removes. The roasts or principal dishes.

Ris de veau. Sweetbreads.

Salade de laitue. Lettuce salad.

Salade de légumes. Vegetable salad.

Salpicon. Highly seasoned minced meat mixed with a thick sauce.

Selle de venaison. Saddle of venison.

Sippets. English for croutons.

Soufflé. Literally, puffed up.

Soupe a l'ognon. Onion soup.

Sucres. Sweets.

Tarte aux pommes. Apple pie.

Tourte. A tart.

✳ – – – – – ✳

MEASUREMENTS

The following chart shows how much measuring standards in cooking have changed in the past century. This chart is from the book *Food for the Sick and How to Prepare It* by Edwin Charles French, M.D., published by J.P. Morton and Company in 1900.

Table of Approximate Weights and Measures

Three teaspoonfuls	*one tablespoonful*
Four tablespoonfuls	*one wineglassful*
two wineglassfuls	*one gill*
two gills	*one tumbler or cup*
two cups	*one pint*
one quart of sifted flour	*one pound*
one quart powered sugar	*one pound, seven oz.*
one quart granulated sugar	*one pound, nine oz.*
one pint closely packed butter	*one pound*
three cupfuls sugar	*one pound*
five cupfuls sifted flour	*one pound*
one tablespoonful salt	*one ounce*
seven tablespoonfuls granulated sugar	*one-half pint*
twelve tablespoonfuls flour	*one pint*
three coffee cupfuls	*one quart*
ten eggs	*one pound*

A tablespoonful is frequently mentioned in receipts [sic]. It is generally understood as a measure or bulk equal to that which would be produced by half an ounce of water.

✳ – – – – – ✳

So what is a gill or tumbler, and how much is in a wineglass? The following lists give the modern equivalents to archaic terms.

LIQUID MEASUREMENTS

4 drams = 1 tablespoon

76 drops = 1 teaspoon

1 gill = ½ cup

1 jigger = 3 tablespoons
1 kitchen cup = 1 cup
1 pint = 2 cups
1 pottle = 2 quarts
1 saltspoon = ¼ teaspoon
1 tumbler = 1 cup
1 wine glass = ¼ cup

DRY MEASUREMENTS

1 bushel = 8 gallons (dry)
1 coffeecup = scant cup
1 dessert or soup spoon = 2 teaspoons
1 kitchen spoon = 1 teaspoon
1 peck = 2 gallons (dry)
1 pinch or dash = less than ⅛ teaspoon
1 saucer = about 1 heaping cup
1 spoonful = about 1 tablespoon
1 teacup = scant ¾ cup

– – – – –

This "Table of Weights and Measures" is from *The Third Presbyterian Cook Book and Household Directory* published in the interest of the Manse Fund by the Mite Society of the Third Presbyterian Church of Chester, Pa. (1917).

TABLE OF WEIGHTS AND MEASURES

"With weights and measures just and true,
Oven of even heat:
Well buttered tins and quiet nerves,
Success will be complete."

4 saltspoonfuls liquid	1 teaspoonful
4 teaspoonfuls	1 tablespoonful
3 teaspoonfuls dry material	1 tablespoonful
4 tablespoonfuls liquid	1 wineglass, ½ gill, ¼ cup
16 tablespoonfuls liquid	1 cup or ½ pint
12 tablespoonfuls dry material	1 cup
1 cup liquid	½ pint

4 cups liquid	1 quart
4 cups flour	1 quart or 1 pound
2 cups granulated sugar	1 pound
½ cup butter	¼ pound
1 round teaspoonful butter	1 ounce
1 heaping teaspoonful butter	2 ounces or ¼ cup

A pinch of salt and spice is about a saltspoonful

✳ – – – – –✳

COOKING TIMES AND TEMPERATURES

Modern ovens allow us to set exact temperatures with the push of a button, but our ancestors cooked first over fires and later over fuel-burning stoves. Cooking times and temperatures listed in old recipes may seem vague to modern cooks. Here are some common cooking and baking temperatures you may encounter along with the modern equivalent:

slow oven = 300 degrees Fahrenheit
moderate oven = 350 degrees
quick oven = 375 to 400 degrees
hot oven = 400 to 425 degrees

What was it like to cook with a woodburning stove? The *Cooking School Text Book and Housekeepers' Guide to Cookery and Kitchen Management* by Juliet Corson, superintendent of the New York Cooking School, first published in 1877, gives a thorough explanation of how to care for the stove, build the fire, and maintain the proper cooking temperature.

How to Clean the Stove.—(1.) Let down the grate and take up the cinders and ashes carefully to avoid all unnecessary dirt; put them at once into an ash-sifter fitted into the top of a pail or keg with handles, and closed with a tight fitting cover; take the pail out of doors, sift the cinders, put the ashes into the ash-can, and bring the cinders back to the kitchen. (2.) Brush the soot and ashes out of all the flues and draught-holes of the stove, and then put the covers on, and brush all the dust off the outside. A careful cook will save all the wings of game and poultry to use for this purpose. If the stove is greasy wash it off with a piece of flannel dipped in hot water containing a little soda. (3.) Mix a little black-lead or stove polish with enough water to form a thin paste; apply this to the stove with a soft rag or brush; let it dry a little and then polish it with a stiff brush. (4.) If there are any steel fittings about the stove, polish them with emery paper; if they have rusted from neglect, rub some oil on them at night, and polish them with emery paper in the morning. A "burnisher," composed of a net-work of fine steel rings, if used with strong hands, will make them look as if newly finished. (5.) If the fittings are brass, they should be cleaned with emery or finely powdered and sifted bath brick dust rubbed on with a piece of damp flannel, and then polished with dry dust and chamois skin. (6.) Brush up the hearthstone, wash it with a piece of flannel dipped in hot water containing a little soda, rinse, and wipe it dry with the flannel wrung out of clean hot water.

How to Light the Fire.—Put a double handful of cinders in the bottom of the grate, separating them so that the air can pass freely between them; put on them a layer of dry paper, loosely squeezed between the hands; on the paper lay some small sticks of wood cross-wise, so as to permit a draught from the bottom; place a double handful of small cinders and bits of coal on top of the wood; close the covers of the stove; open all the draughts, and light the paper from the bottom of the grate. As the fire burns up gradually add mixed coal and cinders until there is a clear, bright body of fire; then partly close the draughts, and keep the fire bright by occasionally putting on a little coal. The condition of the draught closely affects the degree of heat yielded by a given amount of fuel; just enough air should be supplied to promote combustion; but if a strong current blows through the mass of fire, or over its surface, it carries off a great portion of the heat which should be utilized for cooking purposes, and gradually deadens the fire.

How to Keep up the Fire.—As soon as the heat of the fire shows signs of diminishing, add a little fuel at a time, and often enough to prevent any sensible decrease of the degree of heat required for cooking. Keep the bottom of the fire raked clear, and never let the ash-pan get choked up near the grate with ashes, cinders, or refuse of any kind. There is no economy in allowing a fire to fail for want of fuel; if the fire is not replenished until the heat falls below the temperature necessary for cooking purposes, there is a direct waste of all the heat which is supplied by fresh fuel until the surface and ovens of the stove are again heated to the proper degree; whereas, if, when that heat has once been reached, it is sustained by the gradual addition of a little fuel at a time, this waste is avoided, and much of the cook's time is saved. In kitchens where this fact is not understood there is a continual waste of time and fuel, to say nothing of the trial of patience which is the too apt response to a request for the services of the cook when she has just mended the fire, and nothing can be cooked until it burns up.

Degrees of Heat from Fuel.—The advantage which one kind of fuel possesses over another depends upon its local abundance and cheapness. We append the average temperature of a clear fire made of different combustibles, and a table of the degree of heat necessary for various operations in cookery, so that some definite idea of the relative values of fuel can be reached:

Willow Charcoal	600°	Fahr.
Ordinary "	700	"
Hard Wood	800 to 900	"
Coal	1,000	"

Shell-bark Hickory has the greatest heating value among woods; that is, the coals it produces are hotter and retain the heat longer than the coals from soft woods. Soft woods burn with a quicker flame and more intense heat than hard woods, and produce more flame and smoke; they are therefore best to make a quick, fierce fire. Hard woods burn more slowly, with less heat, flame, and smoke, but produce harder coals, which retain the heat, and are consequently the best for long continued cooking operations.

Charcoal is the residue of wood, the gaseous elements of which have slowly been burned away in covered pits or furnaces, with a limited supply of air. Newly-made charcoal burns without flame, but after it has gathered moisture from exposure to the air it makes a slight blaze; it burns easily and rapidly, and produces a greater heat in proportion to its weight than any other fuel.

Anthracite coal is the mineral remains of ancient vegetation which has lost all its elements except a little sulphur, an excess of carbon and the incombustible ash. It kindles slowly, but burns with an intense and steady volume of heat which is exceedingly valuable for cooking purposes.

Coke, the residue of any kind of coal from which illuminating gas has been manufactured, is an inexpensive fuel, yielding an intense but transient heat, and is very well adapted for boiling and for cooking operations which do not require long sustained heat.

Prof. Youmans quotes the following figures as representing the comparative heating values of the above named fuels, but remarks that the actual degree of heat derived from them, under ordinary circumstances, will fall below this estimate: 1 lb. of dry, hard wood will raise 35 lbs. of water from the freezing to the boiling point; 1 lb. of coal will similarly heat 60 lbs. of water; and 1 lb. of wood charcoal, 73 lbs. of water.

Cooking Temperatures.—The following table represents the degrees of heat to which food is subjected during its preparation for the table:

Glucose, or grape sugar, melts	80°	Fahr.
Beef tallow "	100	"
Mutton tallow "	106	"
Stearin "	111	"
Butter "	135	"
Albumen coagulates	145	"
Scalding water	150	"
Starch is transformed to sugar	160	"
Water simmers (after boiling)	180	"
Milk boils	199	"
Water boils	212	"
Moderate oven for sponge cake	220	"
" rice pudding	220	"
Baking heat for ordinary cakes	240	"
" biscuits	240	"
" macaroni	240	"
" meat	240	"
First baking heat for bread	280	"
After five minutes moderate to	240	"
Baking heat for pies	280	"
Baking heat for puff paste	300	"
Frying temperature, ranging up	345	"
Smoking hot fat	345	"
Thick fish filets, fry at	380	"
Croquettes	385	"
Saratoga potatoes "	385	"
Fritters "	385	"
Rissoles "	385	"
Kromeskies "	385	"
Whitebait	400	"
Lard boils	565	"
Oil "	600	"
Heat of open roasting fire	1000	"
" broiling fire	1000	"

This "Time Table of Cooking" is from *The Third Presbyterian Cook Book and Household Directory* published in the interest of the Manse Fund by the Mite Society of the Third Presbyterian Church of Chester, Pa. (1917).

TIME TABLE OF COOKING

Loaf Bread	40 to 60 minutes
Rolls and Biscuits	10 to 20 minutes
Graham Gems	30 minutes
Gingerbread	20 to 30 minutes
Sponge Cake	45 to 60 minutes
Plain Cake	30 to 40 minutes
Fruit Cake	2 to 3 hours
Cookies	10 to 15 minutes
Bread Pudding	1 hour
Rice and Tapioca	1 hour
Indian Pudding	2 to 3 hours
Steamed Pudding	1 to 3 hours
Steamed Brown Bread	3 hours
Custards	15 to 20 minutes
Pie Crusts	About 30 minutes
Plum Pudding	2 to 3 hours

*From
the
Family
Kitchen*

113

PART 2
CH. 7

The Arts of
Dining and Cleaning

Cookbooks have been a wealth of domestic information for generations. In addition to recipes, early cookbooks often included detailed instructions for cleaning (especially the kitchen) and household hints such as stain removal. They also included entertaining advice. Presentation is a major part of any dining experience. Cookbooks were informing and advising women how to appoint their tables in proper and pleasing manners long before Martha Stewart started her domestic empire. This chapter contains excerpts on domestic topics covered in period cookbooks. Your ancestors may have followed these rules, or they may have aspired to them.

CLEANLINESS IS NEXT TO GODLINESS

The following excerpt on kitchen cleaning is from the *Cooking School Text Book and Housekeepers' Guide to Cookery and Kitchen Management* by Juliet Corson, first published in 1877.

General Kitchen Cleanliness.—Never cease to exercise the greatest care in keeping the kitchen clean; it is the best place in the house to recall to mind the proverb that "Cleanliness is next to Godliness." (2.) After attention has been given to all the directions enumerated in this chapter, remember to watch the sinks and drains; flush them several times a day with boiling water. (3.) Take care that no scraps of meat or parings of vegetables accumulate in them to attract vermin, or choke the traps. (4.) Never throw soapsuds into the sink without afterwards flushing it with clean hot water. (5.) Run hot water containing a little chloride of lime into the drains at least once a day in summer, and once in every two or three days in winter, to counteract all unpleasant and unhealthy odors. Remember that the best cook always has the cleanest kitchen.

How to Clean the Kitchen.—Dust down the ceiling and side walls with a feather duster, or a clean cloth tied over a broom. (2.) Sweep the floor, setting the broom evenly upon the floor, and moving it with long, regular strokes, being careful not to fling the refuse about the room, or to raise much dust. (3.) Wash the paint with a piece of clean flannel dipped in hot water, in which borax has been dissolved in the proportion of one table-spoonful to a gallon of water; if the spots are not easily rubbed off, use a little soap, rinsing it off thoroughly, and wiping the paint with the flannel wrung out of clean water. (4.) Wash the window-glass with a soft cloth which does not shed lint, dipped in clean water and wrung out; polish the glass with a clean, dry cloth, or with newspaper. (5.) Scrub the tables with hot water, in which a little washing soda and soap have been dissolved, using a stiff brush; then rinse them with a cloth wrung out of clean, hot water, and wipe them as dry as possible. (6.) Scrub the floor in the same manner, and wipe it quite dry. (7.) Wash all the scrubbing brushes and cloths in hot water containing a little soda and soap. (8.) Wash all the dish cloths and kitchen towels in hot water, with soap and soda, or borax, every time they are used, and keep a clean, dry stock of them on hand.

*From
the
Family
Kitchen*

115

PART 2
CH. 8

These detailed instructions of properly sweeping and dusting a room are from *Student's Manual in Household Arts: Food and Cookery* by Martha L. Metcalf, published in 1915.

SWEEPING AND DUSTING

1. Before beginning to sweep, see that no food is left uncovered in the room.

2. Open the windows and close the doors.

3. Dust and remove chairs, etc. Cover such articles as cannot be taken from the room.

4. Wet the broom in a solution of borax and water. Do not use tea leaves or corn meal. Tea leaves may leave a stain and corn meal is apt to attract water bugs. Small pieces of newspaper well dampened and sprinkled on the floor may be used.

5. Sweep from the edges of the room towards the center.

6. Sweep with short strokes, keeping the broom close to the floor. This keeps the dust from flying. If the broom is properly held it will be impossible to lift it at the end of each stroke and set the dust flying.

7. When the dust has been gathered at one spot, take it up with a short broom and dustpan.

8. Always sweep a floor before washing or scrubbing it.

9. After sweeping a room, dust the woodwork and furniture, bring in the articles that were taken out, set the room in order and partly close the windows.

10. Always use a damp duster, which will collect and hold the dust, instead of merely moving it from place to place as a dry duster or feather duster will do. When the work is completed, wash the duster and so get rid of the dust.

11. New brooms may be soaked in strong, hot salt water before using, to toughen the bristles and make the brooms last longer.

These helpful household hints are from the 1894 book *How We Cook in Los Angeles. A practical cook-book, containing six hundred or more recipes* by the Ladies' Social Circle, Simpson M.E. Church, Los Angeles, California.

» Cold tea is excellent for cleaning grained wood.

» The ashes of wheat straw make an excellent silver polish. Apply with soft leather or chamois.

» Little bags of unground pepper pinned to hangings and among clothes in wardrobes will keep away moths. Ground black pepper sprinkled plentifully into fur will preserve effectually from moths.

» Sprinkle fine meal on grease spots in your carpet. Let it remain several hours and it will have absorbed the grease.

» Tar on cotton goods can be removed by spreading clean lard on the part stained, allowing it to remain for some little time.

» Rub ink stains on linen with clean tallow before washing and boiling.

» To remove grease from silk goods, wash with ether.

Mrs. W. B. A.

» To set the color in any cotton or linen goods, dissolve one tablespoon of sugar of lead in a pail of very hot water. This will be sufficient for 10 to 12 yards of goods. Dip thoroughly, seeing that every part is evenly wet. Keep in the water from 20 to 30 minutes. This will not injure the most delicate color, but fix it indellibly [sic]. If you feel at all doubtful, try a small piece of your goods—dry, then wash in the ordinary way.

» Lemon juice and salt will usually remove rust.

» To take stains from silk, use 1 part essence of lemon and 5 parts spirits of turpentine. Apply with a linen cloth.

These household hints are from *The Third Presbyterian Cook Book and Household Directory* published in the interest of the Manse Fund by the Mite Society of the Third Presbyterian Church of Chester, Pa. (1917).

KITCHEN HINTS

A teaspoonful of butter put into hot water in which vegetables are boiled will prevent boiling over.

Try putting the pumpkin through the meat chopper before cooking. It is easily done and it needs little water to cook, and in a short time is tender. If juice runs through chopper, collect it and pour over pumpkin. If put in the oven to stew, it need not be watched as carefully as if cooked on top the stove, or it may be cooked in double boiler.

A teaspoonful of lemon juice to a quart of water will make rice very white, and keep the grains separate when boiled.

Too rapid boiling ruins the flavor of any sauce. It must boil once, and never do more than simmer afterwards.

Puddings put into a half-heated oven or cooked in water that has been allowed to go off the boil, are invariably spoiled.

When frying bacon, or sausage, sprinkle a little salt at the bottom of the frying-pan before starting, which will prevent the fat splashing about.

When making soup, if there is no time to let it cool, strain it and heat it again before serving; pass it through a clean white cloth, wrung out of cold water. The coldness of the cloth will coagulate the fat and prevent the pure grease from getting through.

Food authorities say to scald all meat before it is cooked. Soda should also be sprinkled over the meat. There is no nutrition lost by this process, and scientists advocate its use in addition to that of scalding water.

THINGS WORTH KNOWING

Carpets and rugs may be brightened by wiping with a cloth wrung out of ammonia water. Two tablespoons of ammonia to a six quart pail of water.

When putting away white clothing to remain for any length of time, wrap up carefully in blue paper or even a dark blue cloth, and it will come out looking as white as ever it was, no matter how long it lies.

An old book-case set on the kitchen table, back to the wall, makes a very respectable imitation of a kitchen cabinet and saves many steps.

To remove iron rust or fresh ink stains moisten with lemon juice, sprinkle with salt and lay in the sun; for ink, the process may require repetition.

Sprinkle borax, with a little sugar, under pantry shelf papers, and also about water pipes to drive away water bugs and roaches.

To drive away ants from the pantry, lay pieces of camphor on the shelves. The ants will disappear.

Boiled starch is improved by the addition of a little sperm or kerosene oil.

When a glass stopper will not come out of a bottle, allow one or two drops of glycerine to soak in, and it can be removed quite easily.

To remove the taste of fish, onions, or any strong scented vegetables from knives that have been used in cutting, dig the blades once or twice in garden mold, and it will disappear.

Kitchen floors painted with boiled linseed oil are very easily cleaned.

A pair of scissors is infinitely better for trimming off the rind from ham or bacon than a knife.

Salt combined with vinegar and heated to boiling point, will restore the polish to brass and copper.

— — — — —

NECESSARY KITCHEN EQUIPMENT

If you spend any time cooking, you probably have a favorite kitchen gadget. Your ancestors likely had their favorites as well. How were their kitchens equipped? The following excerpt from *Cookery and Housekeeping: A Manual of Domestic Economy for Large and Small Families* by Mrs. Henry Reeve (London: Longmans, Green and Co., 1882) gives us some clues:

The lists here given are on a very moderate scale, suitable to small families; more fish-kettles and stockpots, sauté pans and saucepans can easily be added.

COOKING STOVE

Moulds of varied form and shape in tin and copper are to be seen in every ironmonger's shop, and cooks are too apt to ask for new shapes, and to think more of the form in which a jelly or a cream is served than of the clearness of the jelly and the flavour of the cream. But there should be moulds to hold different quantities, quarts and pints, and of course when double dishes are served there must be double sets of moulds. The best grate or hot-plate for cooking purposes has yet to be devised. The old-fashioned open range roasts admirably, but it does everything else very badly. A hot-plate, or gas rings, or charcoal fires in a hot-plate must exist in every kitchen where there is to be varied cookery. There must be a boiler for hot water and a baking oven. In France a combination of hot-plate, oven, boiler and open fire is to be seen in the kitchen of all the hotels, presided over in general by the 'Host,' who is both landlord and cook, and therefore a judge of the amount of fuel it consumes as well as of the ordinary advantages it offers. This hot-plate is never imbedded in masonry, and is always so placed that the light falls on it, a very important point in frying.

LIST OF KITCHEN UTENSILS. NO. I.

Pestle and mortar; 2 baking sheets; 6 dish covers; freezing machine; 2 dessert ice moulds; 1 ice pudding mould; 1 spice box; turbot kettle; 2 fish kettles; dripping pan and ladle; 2 preserving pans; 4 gravy strainers; 2 egg whisks; 2 frying baskets; 1 salamander, bain-marie pan, jelly bag and stand, seasoning box, omelette pan, cutlet pan; 3 cook's knives; 1 pallet knife; 1 large kitchen fork; 6 copper stew pans; stock-pot; 12 enamelled saucepans; 1 boiler; 1 braizing-pan; 3 frying-pans; 1 colander; 6 yorkshire pudding tins; 6 copper moulds; 6 tin moulds; 4 border moulds; 3 larding needles; 2 trussing needles; 2 sets of skewers; 1 saw; 1 chopper; 1 cutlet bat, pasteboard, rolling-pin, flour tub, weights and scales, mincing knife; 2 wire sieves; 2 hair sieves; 2 tamis bats; 2 tamis cloths; 12 wooden spoons; 6 iron spoons; 1 box of French cutters; 1 box of paste cutters; 2 paste brushes; 1 biscuit pricker; 12 patty pans; 2 tea kettles, toasting fork, gridiron; 2 washing-up tubs; 2 wooden pails; 1 zinc pail.

LIST OF KITCHEN UTENSILS. NO. II.

I boiler; I 4-gallon iron saucepan; I 2-gallon iron saucepan; I tin egg saucepan; I small stewpan (iron); I three-gallon saucepan (iron); I quart enamelled saucepan; I pint enamelled saucepan; I 3-quart iron kettle; I pint tin kettle; I large tin colander; I iron dripping pan; I tin yorkshire pudding pan; I 2-quart milk can with cover; 4 iron spoons; 12 wooden spoons; I tin flour dredger; I tin pepper dredger; I frying-pan; I nutmeg grater; I spice box; 2 trivets to hang in front of fire; I chopping board; I chopper; I hatchet (for breaking bones); I thick oak board about 12 inches square for cutting up meat; I wooden flour box; I wooden salt box; I egg basket; I wire salad basket; I hair sieve; 4 pudding basins, various sizes; 2 pie dishes; I china pastry basin; 2 moulds; I vegetable pan; I earthenware bread pan with cover; I bain-marie pan; 6 copper stewpans, in sizes pints to 5 quarts; 3 iron stewpans, in sizes; I iron digester pot, 3 gallons; I copper saute pan; I copper sugar boiler; I copper preserving pan; 2 block-tin jelly moulds; I block-tin cake mould; I block-tin raised pie mould; I wrought-iron omelette pan; I best tin dripping pan; I cradle spit; I iron stand for dripping-pan; I basting ladle; I oval iron boiling pot; I wooden meat screen lined with tin; I best brass bottle jack; I cutlet bat; I meat saw; I meat chopper; I set poultry skewers; I set steel meat skewers; 2 cook's knives, in sizes; I root knife; I dishing-up fork; I set larding needles; I toasting fork; I fluted bar gridiron; I hanging gridiron; I frying-pan; 6 iron saucepans, in sizes; I large iron saucepan with steamer; 2 enamelled saucepans with lips; I box vegetable cutter; I fish slice; I egg slice; I iron tea kettle; I wire frying basket; I tin colander; 2 best tin fishkettles, in sizes; 2 best tin baking sheets; I pair paste nippers; I box plain round cutters; I box fluted cutters; I bread grater; I paste jagger; a salamander; 6 iron spoons; 2 gravy spoons; 2 vegetable scoops; a girdle; I tin funnel; 2 block-tin gravy strainers; I dozen tartlette pans; I dozen mince-pie pans; 6 dariole moulds; I egg whisk; I marble mortar; I hardwood pestle; 3 hair sieves; I weighing machine and set of weights to weigh 14 lbs.; 6 tinned meat hooks; 2 tamis cloths; 2 corkscrews; I jelly bag and stand; I washhand bowl; 2 cinder shovels; I box coffee mill; a mincing machine; paste board and rolling pin.

A refrigerator is a great help during the summer months in preserving many of the necessary articles of food; and without ice it is difficult to make puff paste, and to turn out moulds of jelly, &c. in very hot weather. The cost of a refrigerator ranges from 3£. to 15£. and upwards. It is a miscalculation to purchase one which is not large enough to hold a suitable quantity of ice and the various articles of food which have to be 'kept.'

Care must always be taken to prevent the odour of one edible from being imparted to another, when placed in the refrigerator.

✳ — — — — — ✳

The Art of Dining

Presentation is a major part of the dining experience, and cookbooks from the late nineteenth and early twentieth century often included instruction on proper etiquette for setting the table. The following passages on table setting and serving are from *Student's Manual in Household Arts: Food and Cookery* by Martha L. Metcalf, published in 1915.

TABLE SETTING AND SERVING.

Neatness, order, cleanliness and consideration for others are the principles that should underlie all rules for table service. Even the humblest room with the cheapest of table furnishings will seem attractive if everything is neat and clean and the orderly placing of the utensils and furniture shows that thought and care have been given to their arrangement. It is not necessary to know the latest fad in table etiquette. When at a loss as to the correct thing to do, do that which will be the most convenient and pleasing to your guests. For example—the knives and spoons are placed at the right of the plate because they are used in the right hand—the soup plate is placed on a service plate so that it may be more easily handled—the water glass is filled only three-fourths full so that the water will not spill if the table is accidentally jarred, etc.

Laying the Table.

1. The table should first be covered with a silence cloth made of table felt or a heavy, white cotton blanket or a quilted pad made of two thicknesses of unbleached muslin between which is a layer of sheet wadding. This cloth, as its name implies, is to lessen the noise made in placing the dishes on the table, also, to make the tablecloth lie more smoothly and to keep the hot dishes from marring the table. The cloth should be turned under the edge of the table at the corners and securely fastened with safety pins to keep it from slipping when the tablecloth is put on.

2. The tablecloth should be placed over the silence cloth and should be absolutely smooth, straight and even, with the center fold of the cloth exactly in the middle of the table.

3. A few cut flowers or a small fern or a dish of fruit in the center of the table will add to its attractiveness. Only fresh flowers should be used and care should be taken not to have the bouquet or fern so large as to obstruct the view across the table. If flowers are used, select those that will harmonize with the main color in the luncheon. For example, purple asters would not look as well on the table when the meal included tomatoes, beets and possibly cherries as would a vase of red or white asters or a small fern. A little thought in matters of this kind helps to make housework interesting and keeps it from becoming drudgery.

4. A doily or centerpiece should be placed under the center decoration unless the tablecloth is a pattern cloth and has a figure woven in the center, in which case the doily will not be necessary.

5. Usually all of the silver to be used during the meal is placed on the table before the guests sit down. For an elaborate luncheon where a great many pieces of silver would be needed, only the utensils needed for the first course are on the table, the rest are placed as needed.

6. The plate should be placed right side up, one inch from the edge of the table at each place. The knife (or knives if more than one is used), should be placed at right of plate with sharp edge towards the plate; the forks, tines up, at left of plate. The spoons should be at the right of the knife in the order in which they are to be used, the one to be used first, farthest from the plate. The silver should be the same distance apart and the ends of the handles in line with the lower edge of the plate, one inch from the edge of the table.

122

7. The glass of water is placed at the tip of the knife and the bread and butter plate at the tip of the fork.

8. The napkin should be folded square and placed at the left of the fork with the open corner towards the handle of the fork.

Note.—The plate, knives, forks, spoons, glass, bread and butter plate and napkin, properly arranged for one person is called a "cover."

9. A salt and pepper shaker should be placed between each two guests in line with the upper edge of the bread and butter plates.

10. The gentleman of the house is called the host and usually sits at the head of the table. The lady of the house is the hostess and sits opposite the host facing the pantry door.

11. If all the serving is to be done at the table, the cups and saucers, the sugar bowl and cream pitcher should be placed in front of the hostess and a stand for the coffee on the table at her right. A carving knife and as many

spoons as will be needed in serving the vegetables should be placed at the right of the host. The carving fork should be placed at his left.

12. A plate of butter with butter knife (or butter fork if the butter is served in balls) should be on one side of the table and the bread plate on the other.

Serving.

There are three ways, in which a meal may be served, known as (1) the English style of service in which the food is all served on the table, (2) the Russian style, where all of the courses are served from the kitchen or sideboard, and (3) the compromise style which is a combination of the first two.

The English style is the pleasantest way of serving where there are few guests and not many servants. It adds to the pleasure of the meal to see a genial host skillfully carving the roast and the simplest dessert gains in flavor when dished by the hands of a smiling hostess.

The Russian form of service is to be preferred if there is a large company to be served, provided there are well-trained servants to attend to the wants of the guests. This form of service lifts considerable responsibility from the host and hostess at the time of serving.

The compromise style is usually used at informal luncheons and frequently in homes where there are no servants. It will be convenient to have possibly the salad course or the dessert served in the kitchen and the rest of the meal served at the table.

Suggestions to Be Followed Whatever the Style of Service.

The waitress should see that the dining room is free from dust, well aired, of right temperature (about 70° F) and pleasantly lighted. She must see that everything is in readiness before the meal is announced.

The waitress should stand at the left of the guest who is being served whenever she is passing food from which he is to help himself. At all other times she serves from the right of the guest.

Cups of coffee should be set down at the right, beside the spoons.

Water glasses should be filled without moving them if possible. If it is necessary to bring them closer to the edge of the table, be careful not to touch them near the top.

A folded napkin or a tray covered with a doily should be used to protect the hand in passing dishes. Hold dish low enough to be easily reached by the guests. In passing jellies, vegetables, etc., have spoon so placed in dish that guests may readily help themselves. In passing cream and sugar have handle of cream pitcher turned towards the guest.

Fill water glasses and place butter on bread and butter plates just before the meal is announced.

Have dishes for hot courses hot and for cold food cold. Dishes may be warmed in the warming oven or in hot water. Chill in the ice box for frozen desserts.

All of the dishes belonging to one course are removed before the next course is brought in. Remove the largest dishes first then the plates, etc. Never pile dishes, take one in each hand.

The bread and butter plates should be removed and the table crumbed just before the dessert course.

The glasses of water remain on the table throughout the meal and should be refilled as often as necessary.

✳ – – – – – ✳

Hosting dinner parties, luncheons, and even breakfasts has always been a fashionable activity. Published in 1894, *How We Cook in Los Angeles. A practical cook-book, containing six hundred or more recipes* by the Ladies' Social Circle, Simpson M.E. Church, Los Angeles, offers elaborate menu and decorating ideas for hosting a meal in the home. Whether your ancestors dined in this style or enjoyed humbler repasts, this cookbook offers an interesting peek into high society at the end of the nineteenth century.

A ROSE BREAKFAST—(MRS. EZRA STIMSON)

Decoration

Cloth white; service, dainty as possible; center piece, candelabra with pink shades; careless arrangement of pink roses at either end of the table. At each cover, a half open bud of same rose; the name card, a single satin rose petal. On side table, banquet lamp with pink shade; and scattered about the room, baskets or bowls of roses. The strawberry ice served in real roses, the centers removed and filled. The fragrance and beauty of a "rose screen" is its own reward. Cover a screen with coarse green or pink net; and by use of florists' wire, cover it with roses; unfold and place across one corner of the room.

Menu

Strawberries
Timbale of Shrimps   Cream Sauce
Rolls

Fried Spring Chicken   Peas
Potato Balls   Parsley
Tomatoes
(stuffed with chopped cucumbers, served on cress and capped with Mayonnaise)
Cheese straws
Strawberry Ice   Lady-fingers
Coffee

MAY DAY LUNCHEON—(MRS. M. M. BOVARD)

Table Decorations

From chandelier over table was suspended a large basket of grasses and brilliant May flowers. Dinner cards of dainty little May baskets with salted almonds.

Menu

Amber Soup   Olives
Turbot a la Creme
Lamb Chops   Green Peas
Spring Chicken—Maryland Style
New Potatoes
Luncheon Muffins   Green Apple Fritters
Lettuce and Tomatoes   Mayonaise [sic] Dressing
Strawberry Short Cake   Strawberry Sauce
Candied Rose Leaves   May Baskets
Iced Tea

A MAGENTA LUNCHEON—(MRS. G. WILEY WELLS)

Decorations

This may not be aesthetic, but it is "*fin de siecle.*" As many flowers take on this glowing shade called "nature's red," it will not be difficult to decorate the table with brilliant magenta which is most effective with cut glass, and the satin damask of the cloth.

At each plate, place quite a broad bow of magenta ribbon with a spray of pretty white flowers tied in it. On one loop, painted in silver, the name of the guest and date of luncheon. Have white candles with little magenta shades. Fill bonbon dishes with magenta and white candies. Place around the edge of the cut glass olive dish a circle of magenta pickled beets. Decorate pickle dishes in the same fashion. Another dish with small magenta radishes will add another touch of color.

Menu

Raspberries or Strawberries

Boullion

Deviled Crabs in Shells

(in serving, surround with Magenta petals)

Turkey   Mashed Potatoes

(Use the white meat only—garnish with pickled beets)

Sweetbread Patties   Green Peas

Raspberry Ice

Celery Salad   Cheese Cakes

(Garnish the salad with slices of egg—the whites dyed magenta with beet vinegar)

Charlotte Russe

(Served in small white paper cases tied with narrow magenta ribbon the top decorated with a few candied cherries)

Ices

A brick of Vanilla and Raspberry Ice

Fruit   Bonbons

Coffee

A SPRING DINNER IN GREEN AND WHITE— (MRS. CHARLES FORMAN)

Decorations

Lay the table with pure white napery; placing in the center a large low bowl of Paris daisies with their own foliage. For the ladies, have corsage bouquets of long-stemmed daisies tied with No. 4 green satin ribbon in loops and flowing ends; across one of which write the name in gold to match the daisy's center. For the men's places, write the name on a plain white card, through one end of which pass the green stem of a white carnation with a bit of feather green, for a boutonaire [*sic*].

Menu

Oysters in a block of Ice encircled with Smilax

Salt   Pepper   Lemon   Crackers

Green Asparagus Soup

Baked Barracuda   New Potatoes with Cream Sauce

Sliced Cucumbers

Artichokes with Melted Butter

Roast Lamb   Mint Sauce   Green Peas

Lettuce with French Dressing   Cheese Straws

Snow Pudding

Pistache Ice Cream   Lady Cake

Black Coffee

DINNER FOR OCTOBER OR NOVEMBER—
(MRS. J. H. F. PECK)

Decorations

In the center of the table, place a large cut glass dish filled with purple and white grapes. Tie a bow of lavender ribbon (of generous width) and place on the grapes; drawing the ends of ribbon to the corners of the table, or up over the chandelier. Take small bunches of grapes, crystallized with sugar; tie with ribbons and place at each plate.

Menu

Oysters (raw)

Amber Soup

Creamed Sweetbreads browned in Shells

Olives   Salted Almonds

Orange Sherbet

*From
the
Family
Kitchen*

127

PART 2
CH. 8

CHAPTER 9

Historical Recipes

128

Many cookbooks from the late nineteenth and early twentieth centuries are now in the public domain and have been digitized and posted online. Google books, <books.google.com> and Open Library, <open-library.org> are two great resources for digitized historical books. This chapter contains recipes from both community cookbooks and cooking school cookbooks. The spelling, grammar, and styles have been retained from the original publications.

✳ – – – – ✳

From *King Edward's Cookery Book* by Florence A. George (London: Edward Arnold, 1901).

....

CLEAR OX-TAIL SOUP

1 ox-tail	12 peppercorns
4 quarts stock	1 blade of mace
1 large carrot	salt

I turnip	I lb. lean steak
I onion	I wineglass sherry
2 sticks of celery	

vegetables for garnish: Carrots and turnips cut into shapes with a pea-cutter
Bunch of herbs.

(Enough for 12 or 14 persons.)

Cut the tail into pieces. Blanch, by putting it into sufficient cold water to cover, with a little salt, just bring to boiling-point, then wash in cold water and dry in a cloth. Put into a stewpan with the stock, vegetables, herbs and spice. Simmer gently from three to four hours, keeping it well skimmed. Strain through a hair sieve. When cold remove all fat and clear with the steak finely minced. Strain and return to stewpan. Add the sherry and a few small pieces of the tail and the vegetables, which have been previously cut into fancy shapes and cooked in boiling water.

✳ – – – – – ✳

The following recipes are from *How We Cook in Los Angeles. A practical cookbook, containing six hundred or more recipes* by the Ladies' Social Circle, Simpson M.E. Church, Los Angeles (1894).

BRAINS
Miss M. E. McLellan

Brains; vinegar; laurel leaves; onions; beefsteak; cloves; flower; butter; pepper; salt.

Scald and skin the brains, cover with vinegar; add a few laurel leaves, two or three cloves and a little onion. Let them stand several hours. When ready to cook, pour off the vinegar and stew them in water about twenty minutes. Make a gravy of beef stock, a little flour and butter. Season with pepper, salt and a little vinegar. Put the brains in the gravy and cook them for a few minutes. Serve.

KIDNEY STEW
Miss Delia Clemons

Two beef kidneys; I onion; 4 cloves; ½ pod of red pepper; salt.

Put all together, in sufficient water to cover; boil once; skim; then let simmer three hours, until tender. Next morning, cut them open; remove all fat, and cut in small pieces. Put a large spoonful of butter in a skillet; sift in a little flour; brown; then turn in the kidneys and gravy. Stir until it thickens a little. Serve hot.

IMITATION PATTIE DE FOIE GRAS
Marion Harland

Liver of 4 or 5 fowls and as many gizzards; 3 tablespoons melted butter; 1 chopped onion; 1 tablespoon Worcestershire, or other pungent sauce; salt and white pepper to taste; a few truffles—if you can get them.

Boil the livers until quite done; drain and wipe dry, and, when cold, rub them to a paste in a Wedgewood mortar. Let the butter and onion simmer together very slowly at the side of the range for ten minutes. Strain them through thin muslin, pressing the bag hard to extract the full flavor of the onion, and work this well into the pounded liver. Turn into a larger vessel, and mix with it the rest of the seasoning, working all together for a long while. Butter a small china or earthenware jar or cup, and press the mixture hard down within it, interspersing it with square bits of the boiled gizzards, to represent truffles. Of course, the latter are preferable; but, being scarce and expensive, they are not always to be had. If you have them, boil them and let them get cold before putting them into the pattie. Cover all with melted butter, and set all in a cool, dry place.

This pattie is a delicious relish, and is more easily attainable than would at first appear. The livers of a turkey and a pair of chickens or ducks will make a small one, and these can be saved from one poultry day to another, by boiling them in salt water, and keeping in a cool place. Or, one can often secure any number of giblets, by previous application at the kitchen of a restaurant or hotel.

HAUNCH OF VENISON—Old Kentucky Huntsman's Recipe

Haunch of venison; ½ lb. butter; salt and pepper.

Put the venison in a large kettle, cover with water, and boil until tender; drain off the water, put the butter with salt and pepper in the kettle, set over a moderate fire, and let brown, first on one side, and then on the other. Venison cooked in this way retains its natural flavor, and will be found delicious.

HAM BONES
Mrs. Jessie Benton Fremont

"The Funeral of a Ham." This is the startling name the Germans give their final use of the unsightly "hambones"—too good still to be thrown away, but too ugly to bring to table.

The bone, itself, goes into the soup kettle and from the broth it flavors, they take enough to stew *gently, (boiling fast, kills flavors and hardens meat)*, the shavings of ham that had remained on the bone.

Put these in the broth with a Chili pepper, a very little garlic, soupherbs and a laurel leaf—pungent, but sparingly used flavors, and let them assimilate by slow, steady heat. Then make mashed potatoes into a lining for a pudding-dish (you can also use boiled macaroni) and bake so it will look light and brown, like a potato soufflé. There may be some baking powder to make the brown top crust and sides, or cream, (I really do not know how it is done, but it should be brown and raised like a nice dish of baked mashed potatoes) and set to the table in the dish in which it was baked. It is simple enough—most excellent and *flavorous*, or only fit for a railway eating-station—according to the intelligent patience of the cook.

....

SQUIRRELS
M.B.M.

Recipes for rabbit and squirrel are interchangeable. The large fat California squirrels have tender, savory meat.

Meat should not be allowed to remain in the paper in which it is sent from the market; the paper imparts a disagreeable taste, aside from absorbing the juices. Meat should be cut across the grain of the muscle. If necessary to clean, scrape fresh meat, or wash all over with a clean, wet cloth. Do not place meat in water. Wipe perfectly dry before cooking. Never put meat directly on ice; hang, or place on a dish in the refrigerator, not in the ice chamber.

Salt meats should be put to cook in cold water, fresh meats in boiling water. In boiling water, if more water is required, add hot water, and be careful to keep the water on the meat constantly boiling.

....

TO PREPARE HOMINY
Mrs. Cheever, Waukegan, Ill.

Two quarts wood ashes; 3 gallons water; 4 quarts corn; salt.

Boil the ashes in one gallon of the water for one hour; remove from the fire and add the remaining two gallons; be sure it is cold water; let it settle; skim it and then drain off the lye; put it in a kettle and add the corn. Boil until the skins crack; then drain off the water and wash in several waters, rubbing with the hands until the hulls are removed. Then cook in water with sufficient salt till tender.

LYONNAISE POTATOES
H.F.G.

One quart cooked potatoes; 3 tablespoons butter; 1 tablespoon chopped onion; 1 tablespoon chopped parsley; salt; pepper.

Fry the onion in the butter until it is slightly browned, then add the sliced potatoes, well salted and peppered. When thoroughly heated, add the parsley, and cook two minutes.

The onions may be omitted.

CHEESE STRAWS
Mrs. C. B. Woodhead

One cup flour; 1 cup grated cheese; 2 oz. butter; pinch of salt; a dash of cayenne; water to make of the consistency of pie crust dough.

Roll in sheets quarter of an inch in thickness, cut in strips, and bake in a moderate oven.

JOHNNY CAKE
Mrs. Z. L. Parmelee

Two cups yellow corn meal; 1 cup flour; ½ cup molasses; ¼ cup shortening; 2 cups sour milk; 1 teaspoon soda; a pinch of salt.

Beat the mixture thoroughly, and pour into tins, that it may be an inch or more in thickness, before baking. While baking, after it begins to brown, brush the top with melted butter. This is a great improvement.

Sweet milk and two heaping teaspoons of Cleveland's baking powder may be used instead of sour milk and soda.

MOCHA CREAM CAKE
Mrs. A. E. Goodrich

One cup granulated sugar; ½ cup butter; ½ cup sweet milk; 1½ cups sifted flour; 1½ teaspoons Cleveland's baking powder; 3 eggs, whites only, beaten to stiff froth.

Cream the butter and sugar together; add milk, then flour and baking powder; last, the whites of the eggs. Bake in three layers in a moderate oven.

Filling: Make a scant ½ cup of strong Mocha and Java coffee, reserving 2 tablespoons for the icing; to the remainder, add sweet milk to make one half pint; put this in a double boiler and heat; when cool, stir in 1 teacup sugar; 2 tablespoons flour; yolks of 4 eggs, thoroughly beaten together. Cook 15 minutes, stirring often; when lukewarm, beat in slowly

2 tablespoons butter. Spread between layers and finish top with the following icing: Beat together 1 teacup powdered sugar and white of one egg; add the two tablespoons coffee and beat till light and smooth.

FAIRY GINGER BREAD—For the Little Ones
Mrs. T. W. Brotherton

One cup butter; 2 cups sugar; 1 cup milk; 1 tablespoon ginger; ¾ teaspoon soda; 4 small cups flour, sifted.

Beat the butter and sugar together until light, dissolve the soda in the milk, mix, and add the sifted flour. Turn baking pans upside down, wipe very clean, butter well. Spread mixture upon them very thinly, bake in moderate oven until brown. While still hot cut into squares—with case knife. Slip carefully off.

MOUNTAIN DEW PUDDING
Mrs. J. S. Chapman

One pint milk; 2 eggs; 4 tablespoons cocoanut; ½ cup rolled crackers; 1 teaspoon lemon juice; 1 cup sugar.

Mix the milk, yolks of eggs, well beaten, cocoanut, cracker and lemon juice together. Bake half an hour. When done cover with frosting made of the whites of the eggs and cup of sugar.

MOCK MINCE PIE
Mrs. J. S. Van Doren. Mrs. Baldwin.

Two eggs; 2 pounded crackers; ½ cup sugar; ½ cup boiling water; 1 teaspoon cinnamon; ½ teaspoon nutmeg; ½ cup molasses; ½ cup vinegar; ½ cup chopped and seeded raisins; ¼ teaspoon cloves; 1 teaspoon salt.

Boil all together 5 minutes. Remove from fire. Add piece of butter, half as large as an egg. Then well-beaten eggs. Makes two pies.

CHARLOTTE RUSSE
Mrs. E. R. Smith

Half pound of lady fingers; 2 boxes strawberries; 1 pint sweet cream; ½ cup sugar.

Fit the cakes neatly in the dessert bowl or platter; cover them with the berries and sprinkle over them the sugar. Pour over all the cream which has been lightly whipped, flavored and sweetened. This is a very delicate dessert. Other fruit can be used—raspberries, very ripe peaches, or pineapple.

– – – – –

The following recipes are from *The Third Presbyterian Cook Book and Household Directory* published in the interest of the Manse Fund by the Mite Society of the Third Presbyterian Church of Chester, Pa., published in 1917.

....

MUTTON POT PIE
Mrs. Emma Haslam

To make the dough, sift 1½ teaspoons baking powder and ½ teaspoon salt with about 1 pint of flour, then rub into it 1 teaspoon of shortening, and mix deftly with water. Roll out and cut in pieces of uniform size. Cook 1½ pounds of mutton, neck or any good stewing pieces, from which the fat should be trimmed carefully after it is cut in pieces, until it is quite tender, and then let it cool. Peel 3 or 4 potatoes and 1 or 2 onions. Make a layer of the mutton over the bottom of a pot; slice a layer of potatoes over this, then a layer of onions, and over this lay pieces of the dough, apart from each other. Repeat this until all is used, finishing with the dough. Over each layer sprinkle flour, salt and pepper, and on top of last layer lay a sprig of parsley or celery. Cover with water and cook 1½ hours. Start on slow fire.

....

GERMAN STEW

Have a frying pan very hot with fat enough to merely cover the bottom. Into this place chops, or any pieces of lamb or veal, which must be uncooked. Brown quickly on both sides, and remove from the fire. Put a layer of one half of the chops on the bottom of a baking dish; season with salt and pepper, and on this put a layer of green corn cut from the cob. Sprinkle with a little flour and then add a layer of uncooked lima beans. Repeat these layers from the chops up, and add enough boiling water to reach not quite to the top of the beans. If desired a few sweet potatoes can be placed on top of the stew. Cover closely, and cook slowly from 1½ to 2 hours. This makes a savory dish for lunch or supper.

....

ENGLISH BEEFSTEAK PUDDING
Mrs. Robert Bradley

Line a large bowl with a dumpling dough. Cut in small pieces 1½ pounds of rump steak, season to taste, add onions if desired, and place in bowl. Pour over it one cup of cold water, and cover it with dough, as for a pie. Then cover the bowl with a small plate or saucer, and tie all in a large cloth. Place in a large pot with enough water to come up three-quarters way of the bowl and boil three hours. Mushrooms may be added to this stew, if desired.

SWEET-BREAD SALAD
Mary E. Bonner, Edwardsville, Ill.

2 pairs sweet-breads	3 stalks celery
1 can mushrooms	

Boil sweet-breads dry and cut in small pieces; wash and dry celery, cut in small pieces. Boil mushrooms, dry and mix together with mayonnaise dressing:

2 hard-boiled eggs	½ teacup vinegar
1 teaspoon salt	1 raw egg, well beaten
1 teaspoon pepper	3 teaspoons oil or butter
1 teaspoon French mustard	2 teaspoons white sugar

MOCK OYSTERS
Mrs. J. C. Van Pelt

Parboil a nice veal cutlet. Cut in small pieces, about the size of a large oyster. Dip each piece in egg and cracker dust and fry a nice brown.

STEWED VEAL WITH TOMATOES
Mrs. S. T. Robinson, Edwardsville, Ill.

Brown flour and lard together in a pot, put in the meat, pour over it the tomatoes, strained through a colander, add salt, a dash of red pepper, and a pint of hot water, flavor with thyme. Cook 2½ hours, having only enough liquor left for gravy when done. Serve with steamed rice.

5 lbs. veal ham	1 heaping cookspoon flour
1 large cookspoon lard	¾ can tomatoes

STUFFED EGGS
Mrs. M. Brandt, Fayetteville, N.C.

Cut 6 hard boiled eggs in two lengthwise or across; if the latter, cut a slice from each end, so they will stand up. Mash the yolks fine and add to them a little more than half their bulk in finely ground cooked meat, preferably ham; season with salt, ¼ of a saltspoon of mustard, and 1 level teaspoonful of chopped parsley; moisten to a paste of consistency with cream or raw egg, and fill into the cooked whites, rounding over the tops. Rub with melted butter, place on a baking dish, pour around either a good meat gravy or white sauce, and bake until brown.

Or mash the yolks as above, season with salt, pepper, melted butter and parsley; fill into the whites, rub over with raw white, and press two halves together, making a whole egg; cover with beaten egg, roll in crumbs, and fry in deep fat. Cover the bottom of a hot platter with half an inch of tomato sauce, squeeze the left-over eggs over it (there will only be enough to be decorative) and lay in the eggs. Garnish the edge of the platter with parsley sprigs.

SALMON CROQUETTES
Miss Lydia Eyre Baker

1 can salmon	1 tablespoon chopped parsley
1 cup sweet cream	1 teaspoon salt
3 tablespoons flour	Juice half lemon
1 large tablespoon butter	A little cayenne

Drain salmon—chop fine, add to it the salt, parsley, lemon juice and cayenne. Mix thoroughly. Let the cream boil. Rub butter and flour smooth; stir into boiling cream, stir and cook 2 minutes. Season to taste; stir into salmon, mix well and put to cool. When cool form into croquettes. Roll in cracker dust and egg. Fry as doughnuts.

OYSTER PIE
Mrs. S. M. Pierce

Sift 1 qt. flour, 2 teaspoons baking powder and salt (to taste) together, then work into it 1 tablespoon butter, and 1 tablespoon lard, and mix with ice-cold water. Roll out and line a deep baking dish; fill with oysters, retaining a portion of the liquor, a few slices of cold boiled potatoes, and a piece of butter the size of an egg, cut into small pieces. Cover with an upper crust and bake in oven.

TO PREPARE VEGETABLES
Mrs. John A. Hanna

Have them fresh. Wash well, cutting out all decay. When peeled, let lie in cold water. Always let water boil before putting them in.

Turnips—Boil 40 minutes to 1 hour.

Beets—Boil from 1 to 2 hours then put in cold water and slip skins off.

Spinach—Boil 20 minutes.

Parsnips—Boil 20 to 30 minutes.

Onions—Best boil in 2 or 3 waters adding milk the last time.

String beans—Boil one and one-half hours.

Shell beans—Require 1 hour.

Green Corn—Boil 20 minutes.

Green Peas—Should be boiled 20 minutes in as little water as possible.

Asparagus—Same as peas; serve on toast with cream sauce.

Cabbage—Boil from 1½ to 2 hours in plenty of water. There are two ways recommended for cooking cabbage so that it will be odorless. One is to never allow the water to heat above the temperature that will cause it to simmer gently. And the other is, to drop it leaf by leaf into boiling water and cook until tender. The theory is not to break the cells that contain the odor.

SAUCEPAN TOMATO RAREBIT

Mrs. John A. Hanna

1 onion	½ can tomatoes
½ lb. milk American cheese	Butter size of a walnut

Fry onion in butter until brown. When quite brown and frizzled up, turn in the ½ can tomatoes; grate or cut cheese in small pieces and add to boiling tomatoes and stir until melted and smooth. Serve on toast or crackers.

CELERY JELLY OR SALAD

Mrs. John R. Sweeney

Put into a sauce pan two cupfuls of the white stalks of celery cut in small pieces, a half onion sliced, a few sprigs of parsley, salt and pepper to season. Add two cups boiling water and simmer until celery is tender. Strain through jelly bag. Soften two tablespoons of gelatine in a cup of cold water, allowing it to stand at least one hour. Add strained celery water while hot, stir until dissolved.

Season with paprika and juice of lemon, pour into individual moulds.

RUSSIAN SALAD

Mrs. M. Brandt, Fayettville, N.C.

Cut into small, dice-shaped bits 2 ounces of cooked cold beef, the same of cooked cold tongue, of chicken, and, if you like, about 1 ounce of cold boiled ham—Now put into the bottom of your salad-bowl a little of the beef, and place on top 2 boned sardines, a little of the tongue then the chicken, and again half a dozen sardines; sprinkle ham over the top; garnish around the dish and in the centre with crisp lettuce leaves.

GRAPE CATSUP

Mrs. A. H. P. Clyde

12 tbs. ripe grapes	6 lbs. sugar
1 tablespoon salt	1 teaspoon cinnamon
1 teacup water	1 qt. vinegar
1 teaspoon cloves	

Put the grapes in a kettle with the cup of water, boil until soft, then strain. Add other ingredients and boil until thick. Bottle and seal.

Delicious for cold pork.

MINCE MEAT

Mrs. Lillian Hart Maris

2 lbs. beef and liquor in which 1½ oz. salt boiled 1–3 oz. pepper

2 lbs. rasins, seed them	¼ oz. mace, or nutmeg, ground
2 lbs. currants	½ oz. cloves
2 lbs. sugar	½ oz. ginger
4 lbs. apples—green	2 lemons—pulp and grated rind
½ lb. suet—chopped fine	2 oranges—pulp and grated rind
½ lb. citron, cut in very thin strips	1½ pints molasses
1 oz. allspice, ground	1 pt. syrup from spiced fruits or a
2 oz. cinnamon, ground	glass of jelly

Enough for a dozen or fifteen large pies.

138

MOCK CHERRY PIE

Mrs. E. C. Killin, N. Weymouth, Mass.

1 cup cranberries	1 tablespoon flour
½ cup raisins	1 teaspoon vanilla
1 cup sugar	

Chop cranberries and raisins fine, add sugar, flour and vanilla, mix well together, then add half cup of boiling water.

Cover pie plate with pastry, fill with mixture and cover with top crust. Bake.

RICE PIE

Miss Minnie E. Shaw

2 cups boiled rice	2 cups milk
2 eggs	2 tablespoons of flour
1 cup sugar	

Use whatever flavoring you prefer. Line a pie plate with crust, fill and bake as other pies.

....

PORK CAKE
Mrs. John Hoffecker

1 lb. fat pork (chopped fine)	1 lb. raisins (chopped)
1 cup molasses	1 lb. currants
1 teaspoon soda	½ lb. citron
2 cups sugar	

Pour one pint boiling water on the pork and let cool, then mix all together and add spices to suit the taste, also flour to make rather stiff.

....

BLACK JOE CAKE
Mrs. M. Campbell

Dissolve over fire, but do not boil, 1 cup brown sugar, 1–3 cake chocolate, ½ cup milk, and set aside until needed.

1 cup brown sugar	½ cup milk
½ cup butter	1 teaspoon soda in enough boiling
3 eggs (yolks)	water to dissolve it
3 cups flour	

Cream butter, eggs, and sugar, add the melted chocolate mixture. Then add flour, then the soda, beat well and bake in a moderate oven in three layers. Use the following:

Marshmallow Ising

Boil three cups granulated sugar with enough water to moisten, until it spins a thread. Beat the whites of 3 eggs, add 5 marshmallows and pour the boiling sugar over them. Beat until cool and spread between layers and over cake.

✳ – – – – ✳

The following recipes are from the 1911 community cookbook, *The Stonington Cook Book,* published by the Young People's Society of Christian Endeavor of the Second Congregational Church of Stonington, Conn.

....

SOUP CRELOE
The bones and left-over pieces from one fowl.

½ lb. bacon,	4 peppercorns,
½ veal knuckle,	3 onions,

3 carrots,	6 pieces parsley,
3 quarts water,	2 cloves,
2 stalks celery,	½ bay leaf,
½ tablespoon mace,	1 oz. beef extract.

Cook 1½ hours, strain and add ½ green pepper, 12 small okras, ½ can tomatoes, 4 tablespoons rice, 6 hard-shelled crabs. Cook 30 minutes longer and serve. (To prepare crabs, cut in halves, remove claws, eyes, lungs and stomach, wash in cold water, dry and add to soup.) *Miss Florence Willard.*

FISH CUTLETS

2 cupfuls cooked fish meat, chopped fine,	1 cup milk or cream,
2 tablespoons butter,	1 tablespoon chopped parsley,
Yolks of 2 eggs,	2 tablespoons flour.

Dash of paprika, salt and pepper to taste,

Scald milk. Rub butter and flour together until smooth, add to the scalded milk and stir until it thickens. Add yolks of eggs, beaten light. Take from fire and mix gently with the fish. Add seasoning. (Onion and celery extract may be used if liked.) When cool, form into cutlets, cover with egg and bread crumbs, and fry in smoking hot fat. *Mrs. Jennings.*

BEEF LOAF

2 lbs. Hamburg steak,	½ teaspoon pepper,
½ cup bread crumbs,	½ cup milk,
1 teaspoon salt,	½ teaspoon grated onion.

If liked, add ⅔ spoonful poultry dressing, but in that case do not use as much pepper.

Knead into a loaf, place a slice of salt pork on top and bake 1 hour, basting often. *Mrs. E. W. Doty.*

VEAL, BEEF OR LAMB, EN CASSEROLE

Select a tough cut of meat that contains no bone, like the round. Season with pepper and salt, and dredge with flour. Sear on the top of the stove in the Casserole dish until perfectly brown. In the bottom of the casserole dish, put ¾ cupful carrots, 1 small onion, sliced, 1 tablespoonful of fat, and sauté until slightly brown. Then add 2 cupfuls of brown sauce or boiling water, and bake in the oven until tender, basting often. The last half hour, add 1 cupful of potato balls. Serve in the casserole dish. *Miss Florence Willard.*

ESCALLOPED CORN

I can corn,
2 cups milk,
I cup cracker crumbs,

2 teaspoons sugar,
I heaping teaspoon butter,
Salt to taste.

Stir all together and bake three-quarters of an hour. *Mrs. E. W. Doty.*

TOMATO JELLY SALAD

I can tomatoes,
½ box gelatine,

I quart hot water,
I small onion.

Cook until soft enough to put through colander, then add sugar, salt and pepper, to taste. Put in mould and serve with mayonnaise dressing. *Miss Jennie Trumbull.*

BANANA SALAD

Cut a banana in halves crosswise, dip in the white of an egg and roll in chopped salted peanuts. Put mayonnaise dressing on top and serve on lettuce leaf. *Mrs. James R. Carson.*

SUPERIOR SALAD DRESSING

Beat the yolks of 8 eggs, and add them to a cup of sugar, a tablespoon each of salt, mustard and black pepper, and a grain of cayenne pepper. Add ½ cup of cream, and mix thoroughly.

Boil a cup of butter in 1½ pints of vinegar. Pour this upon the mixture and stir well. When cold, put into bottles.

This dressing will keep for weeks in the hottest weather. *Mrs. Theodore W. Hyde.*

WELSH RAREBIT

½ lb. grated cheese,
½ cup milk or cream,
⅛ teaspoon salt,
A little soda,

I egg,
2 teaspoons dry mustard,
A little black and red pepper.

Place cheese over the fire, and when it begins to melt, stir in the egg. Then add mustard which has been mixed with the milk; also the soda dissolved in a little milk. Add seasoning and stir constantly until mixture is smooth. Serve on crackers. *H. H. Doty.*

From the Family Kitchen

141

PART 2
CH. 9

RINKTUM DIDDY

1 tablespoon butter,

1 pint tomato,

½ teaspoon mustard,

1 egg, beaten lightly,

1 small onion, cut fine,

1¼ lb. mild cheese, cut up,

Salt and cayenne pepper to taste,

Serve on hot crackers.

The tomato must be prepared the day before using. Boil down 1 can tomato; season with butter, salt and pepper; cook uncovered until it is rather thick, and strain. Put butter and onion in chafing dish and cook until brown over the flame, then put in hot water pan. Add mustard to tomato, and add tomato to onion. When hot, put in cheese, stir until melted, and add salt, pepper and egg. *Mrs. A. C. Slade.*

PARKER HOUSE ROLLS

1 pint milk,

1 yeast cake,

1 tablespoon salt,

2 cups sugar,

2 tablespoons butter,

2 quarts flour.

Scald milk, and when lukewarm, add butter, sugar, salt and yeast cake. When dissolved, add enough flour to make batter and let rise. When well risen, add rest of flour, knead and let rise again. Then cut in rounds, butter tops and lap over. Let rise for ten or fifteen minutes and bake. *Mrs. E. W. Doty.*

TEA ROLLS

1 yeast cake,

1 cup milk,

2½ cups flour,

1 egg,

1 tablespoon butter,

1 tablespoon sugar,

½ teaspoon salt.

Scald milk, and when lukewarm, add butter, sugar, egg, yeast and salt. When thoroughly dissolved, add flour and knead lightly. Let rise until double in quantity. Roll out, cut into rounds, butter tops and lap half over. When light, bake about twenty minutes in hot oven. *Mrs. Jennie Weems Brown.*

JOHNNY CAKES

1 cup white corn meal,

3 teaspoons sugar,

1 teaspoon salt,

¼ teaspoon soda.

Stir well together, then scald with enough boiling water to make quite soft. Then take up by the tablespoonful, roll in some dry corn meal on a plate, flatten into a cake, and fry brown in enough lard to cover the bottom of a hot frying pan. This makes six or seven cakes. *Mrs. John C. Moore.*

ORANGE PIE

Juice and ½ grated rind of 1 orange,

1 cup white sugar,

Nutmeg, if desired,

3 eggs,

Juice of 1 lemon,

2 tablespoons butter.

Cream butter and sugar, then beat in orange and lemon until very light; add the beaten yolks of eggs and bake with bottom crust. When done, cover with the whites of eggs beaten to a stiff froth and sweetened with two tablespoons sugar. Brown in oven. *Mrs. Theodore W. Hyde.*

BREAD PUDDING

Soak 1 cup bread crumbs or broken bread in two cups milk until softened and beat until smooth. Then add:

1 tablespoon sugar,

½ teaspoon vanilla,

Yolks of 2 eggs,

A little salt.

Bake fifteen or twenty minutes in slow oven, placing pudding dish in pan of hot water. When done, cover top with jam or jelly, and then with a meringue made of the white of one egg. If desired, omit jelly or meringue, and serve with following sauce:

Put in saucepan 2 cups water and 1 cup sugar. When sugar is dissolved add slowly 1 heaping tablespoon cornstarch mixed in a little cold water. When cooked clear, remove from fire and add 2 teaspoons vanilla. Serve hot. *Mrs. Olga Gilbert Imperatori*

SUET PUDDING

1 cup suet, chopped very fine,

1 cup molasses,

1 cup milk,

1 teaspoon soda,

1 cup chopped raisins,

3 cups of flour.

Steam three hours, and serve with a liquid sauce. *Mrs. Abby Chesebrough Matthews.*

CARROT PUDDING

1 cup currants,

1 cup raisins,

1 cup suet, chopped fine,

1 cup sugar,

1 cup grated carrots,

1 cup grated potato,

1½ cups flour,

1 teaspoon cinnamon,

½ teaspoon cloves,

1 teaspoon soda.

Steam three hours, and serve with hard sauce. *Mrs. George Gould.*

COFFEE CREAM WITH MERINGUES

I pint cream,	½ box gelatine,
I pint milk,	4 eggs,
½ pint ground coffee,	½ pint granulated sugar.

Put coffee and milk together on stove and let simmer, not boil. Then take off and strain through a fine sieve or a napkin. Put back on stove and add the yolks of the eggs and the sugar. Let mixtures get thick as custard, then take off the fire and add the gelatine, which should be soaked two hours before you start the cream. Let the whole mixture cool. Then add beaten cream and whites of eggs. Pour into molds and put on ice.

Meringues

Beat whites of 4 eggs as stiff as possible, add a cup of granulated sugar, and flavor with vanilla. Drop on buttered pan. Bake in moderate oven. When ready to serve, lay the meringues around the cream on platter. *Mrs. E. Williams.*

MAPLE MOUSSE

Whip I pint of cream, and beat the yolks of 4 eggs light. Put in a saucepan a generous cup of maple syrup, stir in the beaten yolks, place over the fire, and stir until the mixture becomes hot and thickens. Take from fire at once and stand pan in dish of ice water and beat with egg-beater until mixture is light and cold, then gently mix with the whipped cream. Pack freezer with ice and salt, using more salt than for ice cream, put in the mixture and let stand for three or four hours. *Mrs. Charles Audette.*

MARSHMALLOW TORTONI

I pint whipped cream,	¼ lb. marshmallows cut in quarters,
¼ lb. maraschino cherries,	I cup sugar,
A few English walnuts,	Flavor with wine and vanilla.

Pack and freeze about four hours. *Mrs. Jennie Weems Brown.*

DELICATE CAKE

I cup cornstarch,	I cup milk,
I cup butter,	2 cups flour,
2 cups sugar,	Whites of 7 eggs.

Rub butter and sugar to a cream; mix one teaspoonful cream of tartar with the flour and cornstarch, and one-half teaspoon soda with the milk. Add milk and soda to the sugar and butter, then the flour, then the whites of the eggs. Flavor to taste. Never fails to be good. *Mrs. Williams Morrison.*

SCRIPTURE CAKE

1 cup butter,	Judges 2, 25,
3½ cups flour,	I Kings 4, 22,
3 cups sugar,	Jeremiah 6, 20,
2 cups raisins,	I Samuel 30, 12,
2 cups figs,	I Samuel 30, 12,
1 cup blanched almonds,	Genesis 43, 11,
1 cup water,	Genesis 24, 17,
6 eggs,	Isaiah 10, 14,
1 tablespoon honey,	Exodus 16, 21,
A pinch of salt,	Leviticus 2, 13,
Spices to taste,	I Kings 10, 10.

Follow Solomon's advice for making good boys, and you will have a good cake. Proverbs 13, 24. *Mrs. A. A. Anderson.*

WASHINGTON CAKE

¾ lb. butter and same of sugar, creamed together,

5 eggs, well beaten,	1 lb. sifted flour,
½ grated nutmeg,	1 lb. currants or raisins,
1 teaspoon cinnamon,	½ teaspoon soda, dissolved in 1 gill cream.
1 gill wine,	

Bake in moderate oven. *Mrs. Atwood R. Brayton.*

AUNT PEGGY'S HICKORY-NUT CAKE

1 lb. flour,	2 teaspoons cream of tartar,
1 lb. sugar,	1 teaspoon soda,
½ lb. butter,	½ cup milk.
6 eggs,	

Beat the cake thoroughly and then stir in a small bowl of chopped hickory-nut meats. Bake in a moderate oven. *Miss H. Adelaide Brayton.*

LADY FINGERS

1 cup sugar and ½ cup butter, beaten together,

1 egg,	¼ cup milk,
1 pint flour,	1 teaspoon soda (level),
1 rounded teaspoon cream of tartar,	1 teaspoon vanilla.

Roll out, cut in strips, roll in sugar and bake in quick oven. *Mrs. E. W. Doty.*

DOUGHNUTS

3 cups of milk,	2 eggs,
2 cups of sugar,	1 cup butter,
1 cup yeast, or 1 yeast cake,	1 grated nutmeg.

Sponge the milk, 1 cup of sugar, and yeast over night—about as stiff as for bread. Next morning add the butter, the other cup of sugar, the 2 eggs and nutmeg, and let it rise again, keeping it as stiff as for bread. When light again, add flour until you can put them on the table to mould. Mould about twenty minutes, cut out and let stand where it is warm until as light as raised biscuit. Then boil in hot lard from five to seven minutes. When almost cold, roll them in confectioners' sugar and let them stand half an hour; then roll in fresh sugar. This will make six dozen, and they are very fine. *Miss Lucy Woodbridge.*

BREAKFAST COOKIES

1 cup sugar,	1 egg,
Butter size of an egg,	2 tablespoons milk,
½ teaspoon soda,	½ teaspoon cream tartar.
Flour to roll,	

Turn cookies in sugar before baking. *Mrs. Charles H. Crandall.*

146

PEPPER HASH

1 large peck green tomatoes,	4 quarts green peppers,
1 large cabbage,	1 quart onions.

Chop each separately, salt well and let stand until the next day. Drain thoroughly, and put into it 2 quarts vinegar, 2 lbs. brown sugar, mustard seed, and cook half an hour. *Mrs. N. P. Trumbull.*

MUSTARD PICKLE

½ peck green tomatoes,	1 head cabbage,
1 head cauliflower,	5 green peppers,
1 bunch celery,	1 quart small onions.

Chop all ingredients except the onions, add 1 cup salt and let stand over night. In the morning, drain and add:

½ lb. mustard,	½ oz. tumeric,
1 cup flour,	1 cup sugar.
3 quarts vinegar,	

Put over fire and boil. *Mrs. John Denison.*

SEA FOAM CANDY

Two cups dark brown sugar. Put in pan and cover with boiling water. Let it boil until it threads; then pour very slowly into the beaten white of 1 egg, stirring constantly. Then add ½ to ¾ of a cup of nuts, and beat until thick enough to shake from a spoon to board. *Mrs. C. P. Trumbull.*

BUTTER SCOTCH

1 cup molasses,

2 cups powdered sugar,

1 cup butter,

Pinch of soda.

Boil until it hardens in water, pour in thin sheets and cool. *Miss Helen Cleveland.*

BOILED HAM

One-half ham or shoulder, ½ cup vinegar, 1 tablespoon dark brown sugar, cold water to cover.

Soak ham in cold water if very salt. Place it, skin side up in the cooker kettle. Cover with water, add sugar and vinegar, and cook slowly one hour over the fire. Quickly place the kettle, covered, in the fireless cooker, and do not open for twelve hours. If the ham is tender, let it stand until perfectly cold, then remove from water, and skin. If not tender, reheat on the stove, and repack in cooker three hours longer.

PART 3

Recipe
Journal

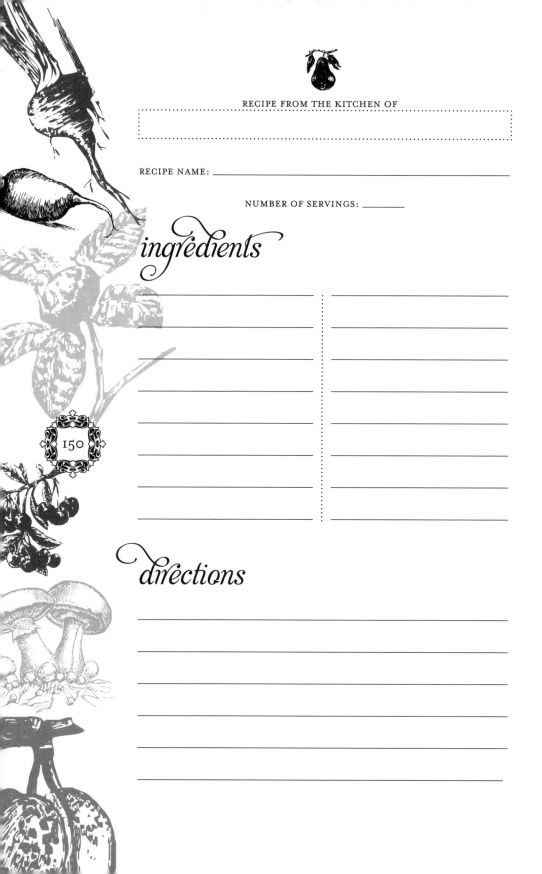

RECIPE FROM THE KITCHEN OF

RECIPE NAME: _____

NUMBER OF SERVINGS: _____

ingredients

_____   _____
_____   _____
_____   _____
_____   _____
_____   _____
_____   _____
_____   _____
_____   _____

150

directions

_____
_____
_____
_____
_____
_____

_____
_____
_____
_____
_____
_____

memories of this recipe

From
the
Family
Kitchen

151

PART 3
RECIPE
JOURNAL

PHOTO OF THE
DISH OR THE CHEF

_____
_____
_____
_____

_____
_____
_____
_____

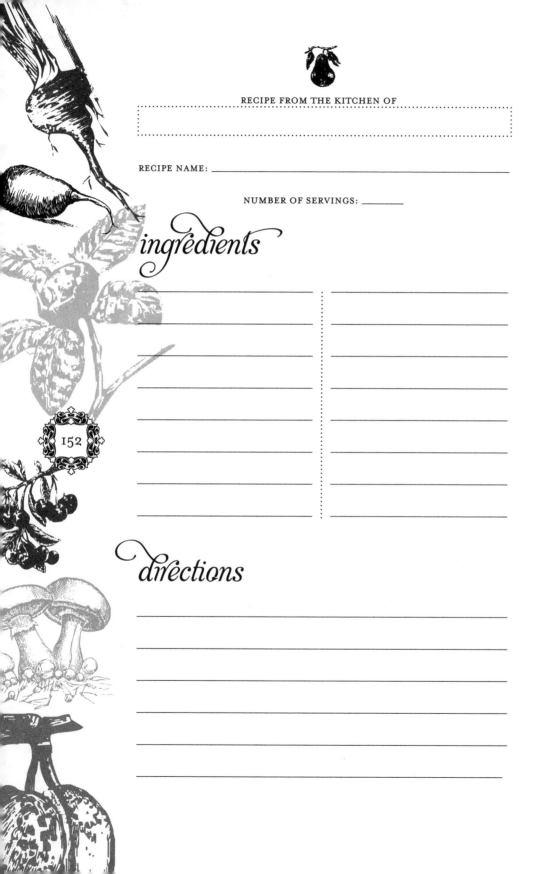

RECIPE FROM THE KITCHEN OF

RECIPE NAME: _____

NUMBER OF SERVINGS: _____

ingredients

directions

152

memories of this recipe

PHOTO OF THE
DISH OR THE CHEF

_From
the
Family
Kitchen_

153

PART 3
RECIPE
JOURNAL

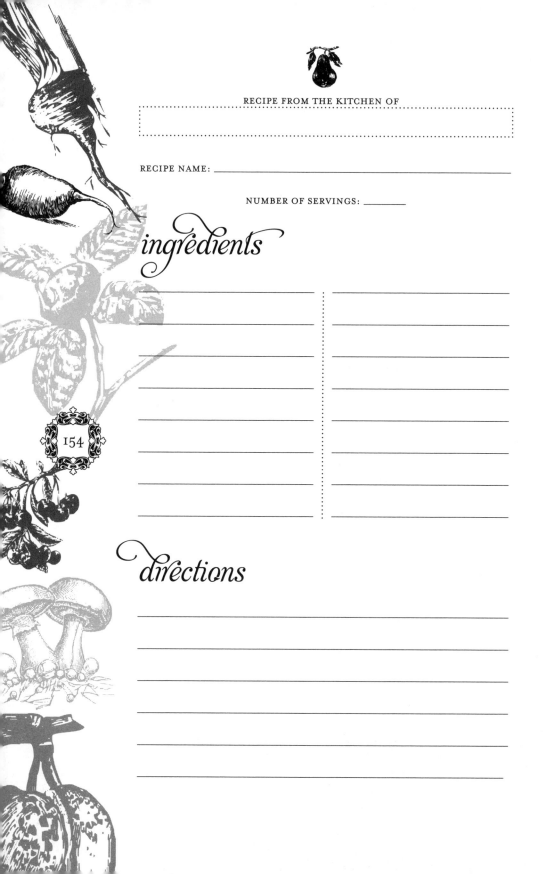

RECIPE FROM THE KITCHEN OF

RECIPE NAME: _____

NUMBER OF SERVINGS: _____

ingredients

_____   _____
_____   _____
_____   _____
_____   _____
_____   _____
_____   _____
_____   _____

154

directions

_____
_____
_____
_____
_____
_____
_____

memories of this recipe

PHOTO OF THE
DISH OR THE CHEF

From
the
Family
Kitchen

155

PART 3
RECIPE
JOURNAL

RECIPE FROM THE KITCHEN OF

RECIPE NAME: _____

NUMBER OF SERVINGS: _____

ingredients

_____   _____
_____   _____
_____   _____
_____   _____
_____   _____
_____   _____
_____   _____

directions

_____
_____
_____
_____
_____
_____
_____

156

_____

_____

_____

_____

_____

memories of this recipe

PHOTO OF THE
DISH OR THE CHEF

_____

_____

_____

_____

_____

_____

_____

_____

*From
the
Family
Kitchen*

157

PART 3
RECIPE
JOURNAL

RECIPE FROM THE KITCHEN OF

RECIPE NAME: _____

NUMBER OF SERVINGS: _____

ingredients

_____   _____
_____   _____
_____   _____
_____   _____
_____   _____
_____   _____
_____   _____

158

directions

_____
_____
_____
_____
_____
_____

_____
_____
_____
_____
_____
_____

memories of this recipe

_____
_____

PHOTO OF THE
DISH OR THE CHEF

_____
_____

_____
_____
_____
_____
_____

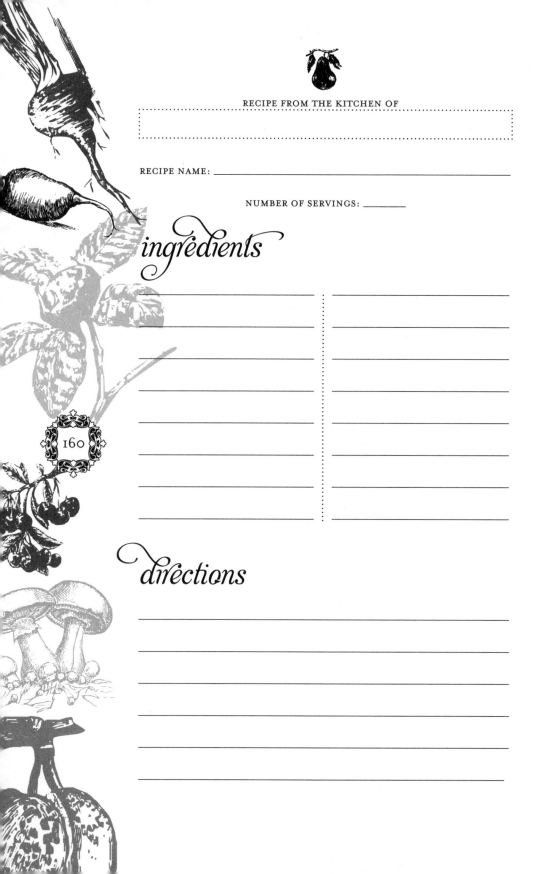

RECIPE FROM THE KITCHEN OF

RECIPE NAME: _____

NUMBER OF SERVINGS: _____

ingredients

160

directions

memories of this recipe

PHOTO OF THE
DISH OR THE CHEF

RECIPE FROM THE KITCHEN OF

RECIPE NAME: _____

NUMBER OF SERVINGS: _____

ingredients

_____   _____
_____   _____
_____   _____
_____   _____
_____   _____
_____   _____
_____   _____

162

directions

_____
_____
_____
_____
_____
_____
_____

_____
_____
_____
_____
_____
_____

memories of this recipe

PHOTO OF THE
DISH OR THE CHEF

_____
_____
_____
_____

_____
_____
_____
_____
_____

RECIPE FROM THE KITCHEN OF

RECIPE NAME: _____

NUMBER OF SERVINGS: _____

ingredients

_____   _____
_____   _____
_____   _____
_____   _____
_____   _____
_____   _____
_____   _____

164

directions

_____
_____
_____
_____
_____
_____

memories of this recipe

PHOTO OF THE
DISH OR THE CHEF

_From
the
Family
Kitchen_

165

PART 3
RECIPE
JOURNAL

RECIPE FROM THE KITCHEN OF

RECIPE NAME: _____

NUMBER OF SERVINGS: _____

ingredients

166

directions

memories of this recipe

PHOTO OF THE
DISH OR THE CHEF

From
the
Family
Kitchen

167

PART 3
RECIPE
JOURNAL

RECIPE FROM THE KITCHEN OF

RECIPE NAME: _____

NUMBER OF SERVINGS: _____

ingredients

_____   _____
_____   _____
_____   _____
_____   _____
_____   _____
_____   _____
_____   _____

168

directions

_____
_____
_____
_____
_____
_____
_____

_____

_____

_____

_____

_____

memories of this recipe

_____

_____

**PHOTO OF THE
DISH OR THE CHEF**

_____

_____

_____

_____

_____

_____

_____

RECIPE FROM THE KITCHEN OF

RECIPE NAME: _____

NUMBER OF SERVINGS: _____

ingredients

_____   _____
_____   _____
_____   _____
_____   _____
_____   _____
_____   _____
_____   _____

170

directions

_____
_____
_____
_____
_____
_____
_____

memories of this recipe

PHOTO OF THE
DISH OR THE CHEF

From
the
Family
Kitchen

171

PART 3
RECIPE
JOURNAL

RECIPE FROM THE KITCHEN OF

RECIPE NAME: _____

NUMBER OF SERVINGS: _____

ingredients

172

directions

memories of this recipe

PHOTO OF THE
DISH OR THE CHEF

From
the
Family
Kitchen

173

PART 3
RECIPE
JOURNAL

RECIPE FROM THE KITCHEN OF

RECIPE NAME: _____

NUMBER OF SERVINGS: _____

ingredients

_____   _____
_____   _____
_____   _____
_____   _____
_____   _____
_____   _____
_____   _____

174

directions

_____
_____
_____
_____
_____
_____

_____

_____

_____

_____

_____

_____

memories of this recipe

PHOTO OF THE
DISH OR THE CHEF

_____

_____

_____

_____

_____

_____

_____

_____

_____

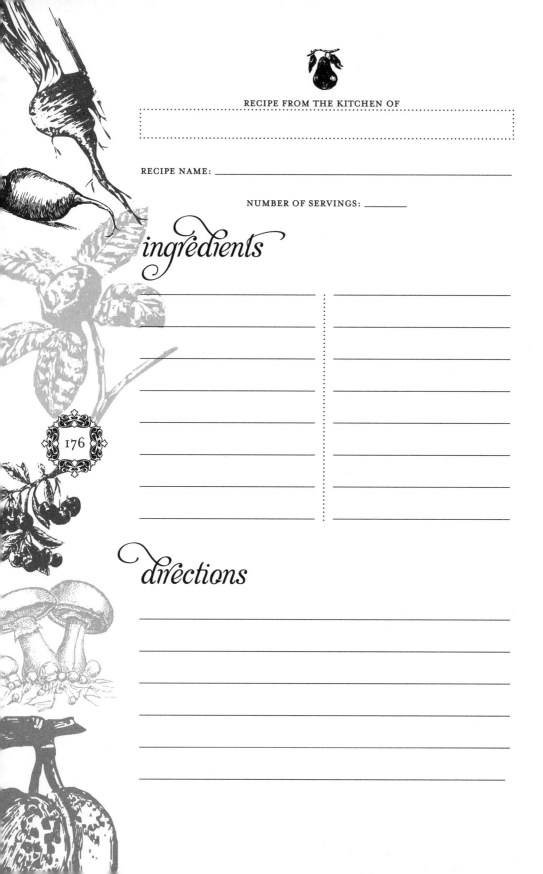

RECIPE FROM THE KITCHEN OF

RECIPE NAME: _____

NUMBER OF SERVINGS: _____

ingredients

_____ _____
_____ _____
_____ _____
_____ _____
_____ _____
_____ _____
_____ _____

176

directions

_____
_____
_____
_____
_____
_____
_____

_____

_____

_____

_____

_____

_____

_____

memories of this recipe

PHOTO OF THE
DISH OR THE CHEF

_____

_____

_____

_____

_____

_____

_____

_____

RECIPE FROM THE KITCHEN OF

RECIPE NAME: _____

NUMBER OF SERVINGS: _____

ingredients

178

directions

_____

_____

_____

_____

_____

_____

memories of this recipe

PHOTO OF THE
DISH OR THE CHEF

_____

_____

_____

_____

_____

_____

_____

_____

_____

RECIPE FROM THE KITCHEN OF

RECIPE NAME: _____

NUMBER OF SERVINGS: _____

ingredients

180

directions

_____

_____

_____

_____

_____

_____

_____

memories of this recipe

_____

_____

**PHOTO OF THE
DISH OR THE CHEF**

_____

_____

_____

_____

_____

_____

_____

_____

*From
the
Family
Kitchen*

181

**PART 3
RECIPE
JOURNAL**

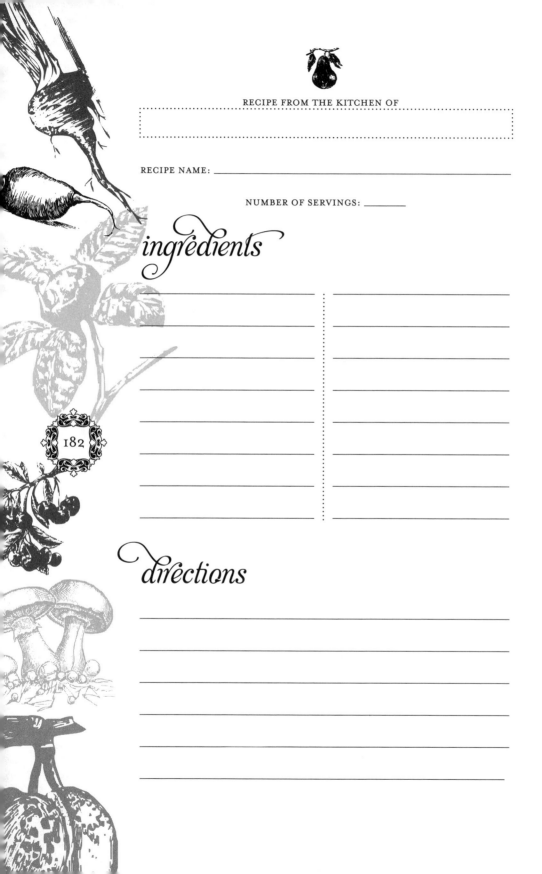

RECIPE FROM THE KITCHEN OF

RECIPE NAME: _____

NUMBER OF SERVINGS: _____

ingredients

_____   _____
_____   _____
_____   _____
_____   _____
_____   _____
_____   _____
_____   _____

182

directions

_____
_____
_____
_____
_____
_____
_____

_____
_____
_____
_____
_____
_____

memories of this recipe

PHOTO OF THE
DISH OR THE CHEF

_____
_____
_____

_____
_____
_____
_____
_____

RECIPE FROM THE KITCHEN OF

RECIPE NAME: _____

NUMBER OF SERVINGS: _____

ingredients

_____ _____
_____ _____
_____ _____
_____ _____
_____ _____
_____ _____
_____ _____
_____ _____

directions

_____
_____
_____
_____
_____
_____
_____

184

memories of this recipe

PHOTO OF THE
DISH OR THE CHEF

RECIPE FROM THE KITCHEN OF

RECIPE NAME: _____

NUMBER OF SERVINGS: _____

ingredients

_____   _____

_____   _____

_____   _____

_____   _____

_____   _____

_____   _____

_____   _____

186

directions

_____

_____

_____

_____

_____

_____

_____

_____

_____

_____

_____

_____

_____

_____

_____

memories of this recipe

PHOTO OF THE
DISH OR THE CHEF

_____

_____

_____

_____

_____

_____

_____

_____

_____

_From
the
Family
Kitchen_

187

PART 3
RECIPE
JOURNAL

RECIPE FROM THE KITCHEN OF

RECIPE NAME: _____

NUMBER OF SERVINGS: _____

ingredients

_____ | _____
_____ | _____
_____ | _____
_____ | _____
_____ | _____
_____ | _____
_____ | _____

188

directions

_____
_____
_____
_____
_____
_____

_____

_____

_____

_____

_____

_____

_____

memories of this recipe

_____

_____

PHOTO OF THE
DISH OR THE CHEF

_____

_____

_____

_____

_____

_____

_____

*From
the
Family
Kitchen*

189

PART 3
RECIPE
JOURNAL

RECIPE FROM THE KITCHEN OF

RECIPE NAME: _____

NUMBER OF SERVINGS: _____

ingredients

_____   _____

_____   _____

_____   _____

_____   _____

_____   _____

_____   _____

_____   _____

190

directions

_____

_____

_____

_____

_____

_____

_____
_____
_____
_____
_____
_____

memories of this recipe

PHOTO OF THE
DISH OR THE CHEF
_____
_____
_____
_____

_____
_____
_____
_____
_____

RECIPE FROM THE KITCHEN OF

RECIPE NAME: _____

NUMBER OF SERVINGS: _____

ingredients

_____   _____

_____   _____

_____   _____

_____   _____

_____   _____

_____   _____

_____   _____

192

directions

_____

_____

_____

_____

_____

_____

_____
_____
_____
_____
_____
_____
_____

memories of this recipe

_____
_____

PHOTO OF THE
DISH OR THE CHEF   _____

_____

_____
_____
_____
_____
_____
_____

From the Family Kitchen

193

**PART 3
RECIPE
JOURNAL**

RECIPE FROM THE KITCHEN OF

RECIPE NAME: _____

NUMBER OF SERVINGS: _____

ingredients

194

directions

memories of this recipe

From
the
Family
Kitchen

195

PART 3
RECIPE
JOURNAL

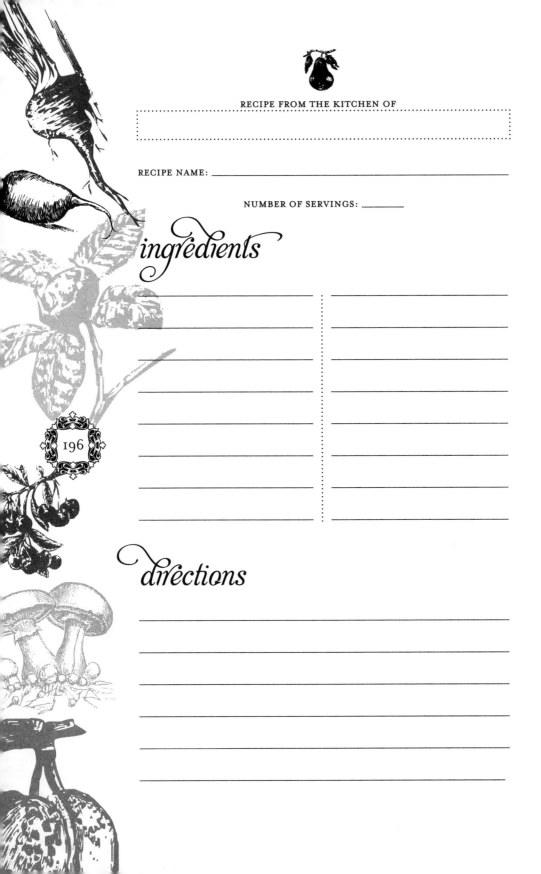

RECIPE FROM THE KITCHEN OF

RECIPE NAME: _____

NUMBER OF SERVINGS: _____

ingredients

196

directions

_____
_____
_____
_____
_____

memories of this recipe

_____
_____

**PHOTO OF THE
DISH OR THE CHEF**

_____
_____

_____
_____
_____
_____
_____

*From
the
Family
Kitchen*

197

**PART 3
RECIPE
JOURNAL**

Bibliography and Resources

COOKBOOKS

» Austin, Bette R. *A Bibliography of Australian Cookery Books Published Prior to 1941*. Melbourne: RMIT, 1987.

» Axford, Lavonne B. *English Language Cookbooks, 1600–1973*. Detroit: Gale Research Co, 1976.

» Cagle, William R. *A Matter of Taste: A Bibliographical Catalogue of International Books on Food and Drink in the Lilly Library, Indiana University*. New Castle, DE: Oak Knoll Press, 1999.

» Cook, Margaret. *America's Charitable Cooks: A Bibliography of Fund-Raising Cook Books Published in the United States (1861–1915)*. Kent, OH, 1971.

» *Cook's Choice: A Selections of Recipes From Rare and Important Cookbooks From the Ninth to the Nineteenth Century*. Philadelphia: Rosenbach Museum & Library, 1982.

» Driver, Elizabeth. *A Bibliography of Cookery Books Published in Britain, 1875–1914*. London: Prospect Books, 1989.

» Driver, Elizabeth. *Culinary Landmarks: A Bibliography of Canadian Cookbooks, 1825–1949*. Toronto: University of Toronto Press, 2008.

» Fisher, Carol, and John C. Fisher. *Pot Roast, Politics, and Ants in the Pantry: Missouri's Cookbook Heritage*. Columbia: University of Missouri Press, 2008.

» Glozer, Liselotte F, and William K Glozer. *California in the Kitchen: An Essay Upon, and a Check List of, California Imprints in the Field of Gastronomy from 1870 – 1932. Gathered from Many Sources*. Los Angeles, 1960.

» Hoyle, John. *An Annotated Bibliography Australian Domestic Cookery Books 1860s to 1950*. Willoughby, N.S.W: Billycan Cook, 2010.

» Lincoln, Waldo. *Bibliography of American Cookery Books, 1742–1860*. Worcester, MA: The Society, 1929.

» Notaker, Henry. *Printed Cookbooks in Europe, 1470–1700: A Bibliography of Early Modern Culinary Literature*. New Castle, DE: Oak Knoll Press, 2010.

» Oxford, Arnold Whitaker. *English Cookery Books to the Year 1850*. London: H. Frowde, Oxford University Press, 1913.

» Patten, Marguerite. *Books for Cooks: A Bibliography of Cookery*. London: Bowker, 1975.

» Reagh, Patrick. *Gastronomy: A Catalogue of Books and Manuscripts on Cookery, Rural and Domestic Economy, Health, Gardening, Perfume, & the History of Taste 1514–1942*. Sebastopol, CA: Ben Kinmont, 2006.

» Streeter, David. *Colorado Cook Books [An Abandoned Checklist]*. Palm Springs, CA: Apoplectic Palm Tree Press, 2000.

» Theophano, Janet. *Eat My Words: Reading Women's Lives Through the Cookbooks They Wrote*. New York: Palgrave, 2002.

» Weaver, William Woys, and Eleanor Lowenstein. *Working Notes: More Additions to the Lowenstein's Bibliography of American Cook Books, 1742-1860*. San Francisco: Journal of Gastronomy, 1990.

WEBSITES

» Internet Archive's Cookbooks and Home Economics collection <www.archive.org/details/cbk>

» Michigan State University Libraries Digital and Multimedia Center's Feeding America <http://digital.lib.msu.edu/projects/cookbooks>

» University of Wisconsin Digital Collections' Recipe for Victory: Food and Cooking in Wartime <http://uwdc.library.wisc.edu/collections/HumanEcol/WWIHomeCook>

FOOD HISTORY

» Elias, Megan J. *Food in the United States, 1890-1945*. Santa Barbara, CA: Greenwood Press/ABC-CLIO, 2009.

» Haber, Barbara. *From Hardtack to Home Fries: An Uncommon History of American Cooks and Meals*. New York: Free Press, 2002.

» McLean, Alice L. *Cooking in America, 1840-1945*. Westport, CT: Greenwood Press, 2006.

» Schenone, Laura. *A Thousand Years Over a Hot Stove: A History of American Women Told Through Food, Recipes, and Remembrances*. New York: W.W. Norton, 2003.

» Shapiro, Laura. *Perfection Salad: Women and Cooking at the Turn of the Century*. New York: Random House, 2001.

» Smith, Andrew F., ed. *The Oxford Companion to American Food and Drink*. Oxford: Oxford University Press, 2007.

» Smith, Andrew F. *Eating History: 30 Turning Points in the Making of American Cuisine*. New York: Columbia University Press, 2009.

» Williams, Susan. *Food in the United States, 1820s-1890*. Westport, CT: Greenwood Press, 2006.

WEBSITE

» Cornell University Library Division of Rare and Manuscript Collections' Not by Bread Alone: America's Culinary Heritage <http://rmc.library.cornell.edu/food/default.htm>

American Regional Food History

» Battaile, Connie. *An Annotated Bibliography and Index of Books and Pamphlets About the Fruits, Vegetables and Seaweeds of Hawaii.* 1975.

» Bower, Anne, ed. *African American Foodways: Explorations of History and Culture.* Urbana: University of Illinois Press, 2007.

» Conlin, Joseph R. *Bacon, Beans, and Galantines: Food and Foodways on the Western Mining Frontier.* Reno: University of Nevada Press, 1986.

» Gourley, James E., comp. *Regional American Cookery, 1884–1934: A List of Works on the Subject.* New York: New York Public Library, 1936.

» Kurlansky, Mark, ed. *The Food of a Younger Land: A Portrait of American Food: Before the National Highway System, Before Chain Restaurants, and Before Frozen Food, When the Nation's Food Was Seasonal, Regional, and Traditional: From the Lost WPA Files.* New York: Riverhead Books, 2009.

» Opie, Frederick Douglas. *Hog & Hominy: Soul Food from Africa to America.* New York: Columbia University Press, 2008.

» Smith, Andrew F. *Starving the South: How the North Won the Civil War.* New York: St. Martin's Press, 2011.

» Stavely, Keith W. F., and Kathleen Fitzgerald. *America's Founding Food: The Story of New England Cooking.* Chapel Hill: University of North Carolina Press, 2004.

» Stoner, Joan. *California Cookbooks: An Annotated Chronological Bibliography.* Sacramento, CA: California State Library, 1982.

» Wheaton, Barbara Ketcham, and Patricia Kelly. *Bibliography of Culinary History: Food Resources in Eastern Massachusetts.* Boston: G.K. Hall, 1987.

» Willard, Pat. *America Eats!: On the Road With the WPA: The Fish Fries, Box Supper Socials, and Chitlin Feasts That Define Real American Food.* New York: Bloomsbury, 2008.

» Ziegelman, Jane. *97 Orchard: An Edible History of Five Immigrant Families in One New York Tenement.* New York: Smithsonian Books/HarperCollins, 2010.

WEBSITES

» Ann Arbor Cooks' Cookbook Collection <http://cooks.aadl.org/cooks/collection>

» Greater Midwest Foodways Alliance <www.greatermidwestfoodways.com>

» Indiana Foodways Alliance <www.indianafoodways.com>

» Peacock-Harper Culinary History Collection's Bibliography of Virginia-Related Cookbooks <http://spec.lib.vt.edu/culinary/va_cookbooks_bib.pdf>

» Southern Foodways Alliance
<http://www.southernfoodways.com/index.html>
» Southern Foodways Alliance's The Creolization of Southern Food
Bibliography <www.southernfoodways.com/images/
Bibliography%20Creolization.pdf>

Religion and Food

» Bishop, Marion. "Speaking Sisters: Relief Society Cookbooks and
Mormon Culture." *Recipes for Reading: Community Cookbooks, Stories, Histories,*
edited by Anne Bower. Amherst: University of Massachusetts Press,
1997.
» Haber, Barbara. "They Dieted for Our Sins: America's Food
Reformers." *From Hardtack to Home Fries: An Uncommon History of American Cooks
and Meals.* New York: Free Press, 2002.
» Romines, Ann. "Growing Up with the Methodist Cookbooks."
Recipes for Reading: Community Cookbooks, Stories, Histories, edited by Anne
Bower. Amherst: University of Massachusetts Press, 1997.
» Sack, Daniel. *Whitebread Protestants: Food and Religion in American Culture.*
New York: St. Martin's Press, 2000.
» Sax, David. *Save the Deli: In Search of Perfect Pastrami, Crusty Rye, and the Heart
of Jewish Delicatessen.* Boston: Houghton Mifflin Harcourt, 2009.
» Smorgon, Hayley, Gaye Weeden, and Natalie King. *Cooking from Memory:
A Journey Through Jewish Food.* Prahan, Vic: Hardie Grant Books, 2008.

WEBSITE

» Brock Cheney's Plain But Wholesome: Adventures in Mormon
Pioneer Food <http://pioneerfoodie.blogspot.com>

Preserving Heirlooms

» Long, Jane S., and Richard W. Long. *Caring for Your Family Treasures:
Heritage Preservation.* New York: H.N. Abrams, 2000.
» Sturdevant, Katherine Scott. *Organizing & Preserving Your Heirloom Documents.*
Cincinnati: Betterway Books, 2002.
» Taylor, Maureen A. *Preserving Your Family Photographs: How to Organize, Present,
and Restore Your Precious Family Images.* Cincinnati: Betterway Books, 2001.

WEBSITES

» Library of Congress' Family Treasures
<www.loc.gov/preservation/family>

*From
the
Family
Kitchen*

201

BIBLIOGRAPHY
AND
RESOURCES

» Minnesota Historical Society's Letters and Paper Heirlooms
  <www.mnhs.org/people/mngg/stories/papers.htm>
» National Archives and Records Administration's Preserving
  Family Papers <www.archives.gov/preservation/family-archives/
  preserving-family-papers.html>
» Western Reserve Historical Society's Preserving Historic Documents
  <www.wrhs.org/index.php/library/preservationprimer>

Conducting Oral Interviews

» Hart, Cynthia, and Lisa Samson. *Tell Me Your Story: The Oral History Workshop*.
  New York: Workman Pub., 2009.
» Ralph, LeAnn R. *Preserve Your Family History: A Step-by-Step Guide for Interviewing
  Family Members and Writing Oral Histories*. Colfax, WI: LeAnn Ralph, 2007.

WEBSITES

» DoHistory's Step-by-Step Guide to Oral History
  <http://dohistory.org/on_your_own/toolkit/oralHistory.html>
» Smithsonian Institution's Folklife and Oral History Interviewing Guide
  <www.folklife.si.edu/resources/pdf/interviewingguide.pdf>

Writings About Food and Family

» Berzok, Linda Murray, ed. *Storied Dishes: What Our Family Recipes Tell Us
  About Who We Are and Where We've Been*. Santa Barbara, CA: Praeger, 2011.
» Ehrlich, Elizabeth. *Miriam's Kitchen: A Memoir*. New York: Viking, 1997.
» Inness, Sherrie A., ed. *Pilaf, Pozole, and Pad Thai: American Women and Ethnic
  Food*. Amherst: University of Massachusetts, 2001.
» Schenone, Laura. *The Lost Ravioli Recipes of Hoboken: A Search for Food and Family*.
  New York: Norton & Co., 2008.

Creating Scrapbooks and Cookbooks

» Higgins, Becky. *Family History Scrapbooking*. Escondido, CA: Primedia,
  2006.
» Jacob, Dianne. *Will Write for Food: The Complete Guide to Writing Cookbooks, Blogs,
  Reviews, Memoir, and More*. Cambridge, MA: Da Capo Lifelong, 2010.
» Taylor, Maureen A. *Scrapbooking Your Family History*. Cincinnati:
  Betterway Books, 2003.
» Whipple, Wendy A. Bougher. *Creating an Heirloom: Writing Your
  Family's Cookbook*. Baltimore: PublishAmerica, 2005.

» Wolfe, J. Kevin. *You Can Write a Cookbook*. Cincinnati: Writer's Digest Books, 2000.

Menus
» Clarkson, Janet. *Menus From History: Historic Meals and Recipes for Every Day of the Year*. Santa Barbara, CA: Greenwood Press, 2009.

WEBSITES
» Alice Statler Library's Menu Collection
   <www.ccsf.edu/Library/alice/menucollection.html>
» American Antiquarian Society's Menus
   <www.americanantiquarian.org/menus.htm>
» Cornell's School of Hotel Administration Restaurant
   Menus Database Search <www.hotelschool.cornell.edu/research/
   library/collections/menus/>
» The Culinary Institute of America's Menu Collections
   <www.ciachef.edu/newyork/library/menus.asp>
» Los Angeles Public Library Menu Collection
   <http://www.lapl.org/resources/en/menu_collection.html>
» New York Public Library's Menu Collection Research Guide
   <http://legacy.www.nypl.org/research/chss/grd/resguides/menus/>
» University of Nevada Las Vegas Libraries' Menu Collections
   <http://library.nevada.edu/speccol/menus/index.html>
» University of Washington Menus Collection
   <http://content.lib.washington.edu/menusweb/index.html>

Genealogy
» Morgan, George G. *How to Do Everything Genealogy*. New York: McGraw-Hill, 2009.
» Rising, Marsha Hoffman. *The Family Tree Problem Solver: Tried-and-True Tactics for Tracing Elusive Ancestors*. Cincinnati: Family Tree Books, 2011.
» Sturdevant, Katherine Scott. *Bringing Your Family History to Life Through Social History*. Cincinnati: Betterway Books, 2000.

WEBSITES
» Ancestry.com <www.ancestry.com>
» FamilySearch <www.familysearch.org>
» Cyndi's List of Genealogy Sites on the Internet <www.cyndislist.com>

Index

204

From
the
Family
Kitchen

205

BIBLIOGRAPHY
AND
RESOURCES

About the Author

Gena Philibert-Ortega holds master's degrees in interdisciplinary studies and religion. She is the author of *Putting the Pieces Together* and the *Cemeteries of the Eastern Sierra* (Arcadia Publishing) and editor of the *Utah Genealogical Association's Crossroads Magazine*. She instructs genealogy and social media courses at the National Institute for Genealogical Studies and directs GenealogyWise <genealogywise.com>. Gena serves as vice-president for the Southern California Chapter of the Association of Professional Genealogists and a director for the California State Genealogical Alliance. She blogs at Gena's Genealogy <philibertfamily.blogspot.com> and Food.Family.Ephemera <foodfamilyephemera.blogspot.com>.

Acknowledgments

It is a long-standing tradition to acknowledge that a book is a group effort. To say that about this book would be an understatement. Aside from the people who answered questions over library website chats, entertained rhetorical questions at conferences, and shared their food histories with me without realizing my interest, there are those who helped me in other ways.

I want to thank my friend Madaleine Laird who first encouraged me to pursue the subject of food, genealogy, and community cookbooks. She was there when I said, "Hey, I've got an idea" and encouraged me to pursue it. She helped find information, went on book crawls, and fleshed out ideas that are found in this book.

You could have knocked me over with a feather when my editor, Jacqueline Musser, contacted me about this book and asked if I would be interested. To her and the staff at F+W Media, thanks for your help, encouragement, and support. It's a dream come true to write for a publishing company that I have long admired.

I want to give a special thanks to genealogist Anna Dalhaimer Bartkowski who allowed me to reprint a recipe and information from her family history, *Value Meals on the Volga*. Her book is available at <http://infiniteadventure.weebly.com/value-meals-on-the-volga.html>.

Thanks to genealogist Debbe Hagner for providing ideas and resources. Debbe knew of my interest in cookbooks and shared articles and some of her family history. A special thanks to *Association of Professional Genealogists Quarterly* (*APGQ*) Editor Matt Wright who was interested in my article on community cookbooks and published it in the September 2001 issue of *APGQ*. Portions of that article appear in chapter six of this book.

My family has been a big part of this book from the beginning. They have accompanied me to conferences, tried unusual foods, and located and acquired cookbooks and historical materials. This project allowed us to add to our family history. Thanks to my parents, Larry and Bonita Philibert, for answering questions about their food history and finding historical cookbooks. Thanks to my brother and his family, Jason and Teresa Philibert and son Nicolau, for sharing food and family history that included calling family in other parts of the world, which is reflected in this book.

And most of all, thanks to my family—my husband, David Ortega, for providing advice and letting me bounced ideas off of him, and my sons, Daniel and Brandon, who endured what many children of genealogists endure—being dragged to countless libraries and conferences where they heard a lot about dead people. Their love and support helps me record the history of our ancestors.

Distributed in Canada by Fraser Direct
100 Armstrong Avenue
Georgetown, Ontario, Canada
L7G 5S4
Tel: (905) 877-4411

Distributed in the U.K. and Europe by
F&W Media International, LTD
Brunel House, Forde Close,
Newton Abbot, TQ12 4PU, UK
Tel: (+44) 1626 323200,
Fax (+44) 1626 323319
E-mail: enquiries@fwmedia.com

Distributed in Australia by
Capricorn Link
P.O. Box 704, Windsor,
NSW 2756 Australia
Tel: (02) 4577-3555

16 15 14 13 12   5 4 3 2 1

ISBN: 978-1-4403-1827-6

PUBLISHER/EDITORIAL DIRECTOR: Allison Dolan

EDITOR: Jacqueline Musser

DESIGNER: Christy Miller

PRODUCTION COORDINATOR: Mark Griffin

FREE DOWNLOAD

KEEPSAKE RECIPE CARDS

Share your favorite recipes with loved ones
using these beautiful recipe cards.
Visit **<familytreeuniversity.com/recipe-card>**

FAMILY
TREE
BOOKS

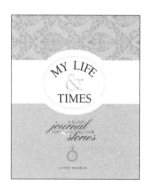

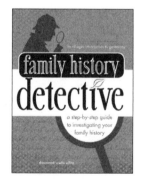